51697

HIGHLAND PERTHSHIRE

"There are more things in Heaven
and earth, Horatio, than are dreamt
of in your philosophy. But come . . ."

"Hamlet"

A

HIGHLAND PERTHSHIRE

Written and Photographed
by
DUNCAN FRASER
M.A., F.S.A.SCOT.

STANDARD PRESS MONTROSE

1976

By the same author:

EDINBURGH IN OLDEN TIMES
GLEN OF THE ROWAN TREES
EAST COAST OIL TOWN

First published 1969
Second edition 1971
Third edition 1973
Fourth edition 1976

941·32

SC941.28
1D

Printed at the Standard Press
Montrose, Scotland

MY THANKS are due to many people and especially to Mr James Morrison, Montrose, who painted the Falls of Dochart for the jacket; Mr Stuart Maxwell, National Museum of Antiquities of Scotland; Mr W. A .Thorburn, Keeper of the United Services Museum, Edinburgh Castle; and the staff of the School of Scottish Studies, University of Edinburgh.

I am indebted to Mr Malcolm Murray, Department of Prehistoric Archaeology, University of Edinburgh, for permission to use his photographs of the Cailliche (p. 40) and Taigh-nam-Bodach (p. 43); the Keeper of the British Museum for the Glenlyon Brooch (p. 51); the Keeper of the National Museum of Antiquities of Scotland for the Clach na Brataich (p. 77), the Dull stone (p. 101), the Quigrich (pp. 122 & 123), the Bernane (p. 130) and the Guthrie Bell and Kilmichael-Glassary Bell Shrine (p. 131); the Scottish Tourist Board for Loch Rannoch (p. 85); the Factor, Blair Castle, for Blair Castle (p. 92); the Keeper of the United Services Museum, Edinburgh Castle, for the Highland officer and his wife (p. 112) and Farquhar Shaw (p. 115); and Mr F. D. Cuninghame for The Black Watch Memorial (p. 110). The Crown copyright photograph of the Honours of Scotland (p. 97) is reproduced by permission of the controller of H.M. Stationery Office and the photographs of St Fillan's healing stones (pp. 120 & 121) are from the files of the School of Scottish Studies. I am also indebted to the Clan Donnachaidh Society for permission to reproduce the Clach na Brataich (p. 77) and to the Postmaster-General for permission to reproduce the Wade Bridge postage stamp (p. 114).

A *

Contents

Nine centuries have passed since Birnam Wood went marching to Dunsinane

1
Through the Gateway

Dunkeld Bridge

ON THE Great North Road that runs from Perth through the heart of the Highlands to Inverness, there is a little town called Birnam, set in the midst of magnificent scenery on the bank of the Tay. Shakespeare gave it a place in history, when he described in "Macbeth" how Birnam Wood went marching to Dunsinane, to fulfil a witches' prophecy. If you go down to the river bank behind the village, you will still see at least one tree from which the soldiers could have torn the branches they carried on that famous occasion nine hundred years ago—a gigantic oak whose massive limbs rest wearily on crutches. Close beside it is a sycamore, not quite as old but ancient enough by any other standard.

These two giants are not the only memories of Birnam's past. The wooded hills, that come jostling down to the river, recall that here you have reached what has been for centuries the principal Gateway to the Highlands. The youngster from beyond Birnam is still something of a foreigner to the city schoolboy, down in Perth. He was much more so in bygone days. If time had been able to take you back 250 years, to the beginning of the eighteenth century when the clans were a living force, you

Beside the Birnam oak is a sycamore, not quite as old but ancient enough
by any other standard

The ell, the old Scottish standard of measure, can still be seen on a wall near Dunkeld Cathedral.

would have found when you crossed the Tay by the bridge from Birnam into the neighbouring town of Dunkeld that you had moved out of one world into another which was quite incredibly different. Behind, you had left a land where clothes were hodden grey and the people unco guid. Ahead was a land where everyone wore the tartan and the folk — as any Lowlander would tell you — were unco bad.

It was tartan all the way in the streets of Dunkeld and plenty of it, for the men still wore the old voluminous belted plaid that was suitable for so many occasions. To see the town at its busiest you had to go there on St Columba's Day in the month of June, when the great annual fair was held. That day the country folk came flocking from their Highland glens to sell their bales of cloth to Lowland buyers from far and near. And the Highland women came too with their tartan plaids fastened in front by a brooch — the married ones with a white linen cloth round their forehead and down to the back of their neck; the unmarried ones with a ribbon, a snood; there was no need to look for a wedding ring.

Occasionally the crowd on the cobbled street would move aside for a moment to let a horseman pass—in tartan truis, with his plaid hanging from his shoulder — and then they would close in again behind him.

If they had been wearing their clan tartans you could have made a shrewd guess how far each Highlander had come to the Fair. Here was a Campbell from around Loch Tay or Glenlyon, and there was a Menzies from the Aberfeldy district. This Robertson, douce and quiet, probably came from eastwards above Blairgowrie. The Robertsons of Rannoch were a wilder, more headstrong lot. And here was a MacNab from around Killin and a Campbell whose ancestors were all McGregors—though most of the folk in Dunkeld that day were Stewarts. A very large part of Highland Perthshire was Stewart country. But you could not tell their clans from their tartans. Two and a half centuries ago, all the clan tartans we know today were still uninvented.

Even among Lowlanders, Dunkeld was a town with a reputation for honest dealing. The dealers had to be honest, for they were all members of the local Chapmen Society and by its rules their measures were checked before they could do any business on St Columba's Day. You can still see the old Scots metal gauge that was used as their standard ell. Measuring an eighth of an inch more than the 37-inch ell, to let the measuring sticks slip in, it hangs on the wall of a house at the Cross. The date 1706 is on it. But the Chapmen Society of Dunkeld and its rules were in existence for centuries before that.

Any Lowlander, of course, was perfectly safe in this Highland town on St Columba's Day or

[11]

The tomb of Bishop
Robert de Cardeny
in the nave of
Dunkeld Cathedral.

any other day. And the same was true if he ventured peaceably up among the hills. He would get food and lodging free of charge at any Highland cottage. But he would always feel like a stranger in a strange land. He would never really get to know those Highlanders—unless he could speak the Gaelic. That was one of the things which struck you, when you reached this Gateway to the Highlands. As you came up from the south, everyone you met was speaking broad Scots until you crossed the bridge from Birnam into Dunkeld. But here the language was Gaelic and few knew anything else. You had come into a foreign land — foreign in customs and traditions as well as language — when you crossed that bridge.

It may seem just a little surprising, if the Highlanders were really as bad as their reputation, that at the end of the main street there is a lovely old cathedral with lawns stretching down to the river. St Columba is said to have spent six months there and founded the original monastery in 570 A.D. Dunkeld was Dun Chaillean in his day and the capital of the Caledonians' kingdom. Three centuries later, when Iona was no longer safe from the Viking sea rovers, the sacred relics of Columba were removed from Iona and reburied here. But one

bone was left unburied—for medicinal reasons. Many a person, grievously sick of the plague, cried out for a draught of water into which this sacred relic had been dipped. And by all accounts it had still not lost its potency nine hundred years later. In the year 1500 an outbreak of plague in the parish of Caputh sent the Bishop hurrying there. He visited the victims personally, had the sacraments administered to them and then made the journey back that night to Dunkeld. Next day he filled a container with water and, having stirred it with St Columba's bone, sent his Chancellor with it to Caputh for the people to drink. "Many drank it and recovered," the Bishop's biographer tells us, "but one insolent fellow replied to the Chancellor, 'Why does our Bishop send us water to drink? I wish he had sent me instead a pot of his best ale.' But he, along with the others who did not drink the water, died of the pest and thirty of them were buried in one grave."

Most of the present cathedral was built in two stages in the Middle Ages. The choir, now used as the parish church, was finished by Bishop Sinclair, in the time of King Robert the Bruce, and the nave was planned a century later by Bishop Cardeny, who died several years before it was finished. There was a couthy

After the great fire of 1689 a new town of little houses began to take shape,
straggling uphill from the Cathedral.

"Even the roof was off before the lairds decided they had done enough."

custom in those days that, when a very well loved bishop died, they carved a life-size effigy and laid it on his tomb to keep the memory of him alive. The effigies of both these bishops still survive in the cathedral, though one is now headless and the other weatherworn.

Enough of the building remains to show us how magnificent it was — the nave with its massive pillars and its side aisles once divided into chapels; the great west window, still with fragments of its once flamboyant tracery; the tower with its mural paintings; and the choir, which has still not lost its thirteenth century character, though the bishop's throne and the chapter stalls and the wide steps leading up to the high altar have long since vanished as completely as the magnificent brass lecterns that a later bishop provided.

They built proudly in those days, not counting the hazards, and these were many. One of the litanies they used to recite in this cathedral was: "From caterans and robbers, from wolves and all wild beasts, Lord deliver us." And a wolf lies buried in the cathedral. But the worst of all evils that befell it came not from wild beasts or Highland caterans or foreign armies, but from three douce Godly noblemen in Edinburgh, who turned its grandeur into a ruin. They issued the orders to

two local lairds at the start of the Reformation: "We pray yow faill not to pass incontinent to the kyrk of Dunkeld, and tak doun the haill images thereof, and bring furth to the kyrk-zard, and burn thaym oppinly. And siclyk cast doun the altaris, and purge the kyrk of all kind of monuments of idolatrye. And this ze fail not to do, as ze will do us singular empleseur." They added a footnote that the windows and doors should be in no way damaged. But who bothers about footnotes! Even the roof was off before the lairds decided they had done enough. Later it was found they had done too much. The choir had to be reroofed in 1600 to provide a parish church. But the nave still remains open to the sky.

There was violence again during the Jacobite rising of 1689. Government troops had seized the town and left a Colonel Cleland in charge of a party of raw Cameronian recruits. And then, one August morning just after the battle of Killiecrankie, the Highlanders returned. The Lowland garrison withdrew to the only building likely to offer any protection, the thick-walled cathedral. Their colonel was killed. He lies buried at the west end of the nave. But the fighting and sniping went on ineffectually until late that evening, with the Highlanders still firmly established in the town. An old Gaelic custom proved their undoing. Back home they were not in the habit of locking their doors and as night began to fall many a house in Dunkeld had Highland soldiers inside and the keys still on the outside. Then the Cameronians crept out from the cathedral and down the close to the town, and locking the house doors they set the thatched roofs alight. The flames spread like wildfire. In one house, it is said, sixteen Highlandmen were burned alive and only the cathedral with three buildings near it escaped destruction. So, in the latter years of the seventeenth century, a new town of little houses began to take shape, straggling uphill from the cathedral towards the mansion of the powerful Earl of Atholl. Those "little houses", now almost three hundred years old and beautifully restored by the National Trust for Scotland, still help to give Dunkeld its very special character.

But we are forgetting about the wolf in the cathedral. It seems just a little unfair that Time has been so unkind to the effigies of the bishops who planned the choir and the nave. It has left one of them headless and the other decayed, and it has laid a much more gentle hand on another ancient monument in this cathedral— the magnificent sarcophagus of a royal prince at the east end of the choir. The four sides of the sarcophagus are ornately carved and on top lies his polished effigy — with a lion at his feet, the hall-mark of a Crusader, a true Christian soldier. This was one memorial which survived the Reformation unharmed. The only damage that it ever suffered was from the King's own soldiers — those same Cameronians — in 1689. They broke his effigy and smashed its Latin inscription. But the wording is said to have been: "Here lies of goodly memory Alexander Stewart, Earl of Buchan and Lord of Badenoch, who died 24 Novemb. 1394."

Though this was a son of King Robert II, writers of old were never quite sure which of them was this prince "of goodly memory". Some said the second son, others the third and others the fourth. But on one point they were all agreed—that on any summing up he was the worst son of that Scottish king. Most of his life was spent far from the hothouse atmosphere of Court intrigue, as a paramount chief in the heart of the wildest Highlands, at his castle of Ruthven on the bank of the Spey in Badenoch. There he was known not as Prince Alexander but as Alister More Mac an Righ, uncrowned ruler of the Highlands. Few people in Scotland were quite as famous, though certainly he was no saint and the only crusade on which he ever went was a somewhat personal one against the church itself. He was

Above.—At the prince's feet is a lion, the hall-mark of a rather special crusader. And Prince Alexander was undoubtedly special.

"Alexander the Great, son of the King."

The gable-ends of old Garth Castle have disappeared in its reconstruction

Garth Castle
at the middle
of last century.

the Wolf of Badenoch, who shocked the godly and the ungodly alike with his wild destructive forays. The Cathedral of Elgin, the pride of the north, was pillaged and left in flames in one of his raids. No one was safe and nothing was sacred when the Wolf was on the prowl.

Elgin Cathedral had been lying in ruins for four years, when the Wolf died and was buried at Dunkeld in 1394—beside the high altar, as was only right for a noble prince of the blood royal. And yet it must be admitted that, to the expert on medieval armour, there is something not quite right about his green marble effigy, fully seven feet long. You don't expect to find fan-shaped elbow pieces on the armour of a prince who died in 1394. The Wolf of Badenoch had been dead a quarter of a century before these came into fashion. People have argued that because of this the sarcophagus cannot be his at all. But others besides the Wolf have had memorials erected a quarter-of-a-century after their death.

It was a long journey from Badenoch to Dunkeld, but the Wolf had other lands much nearer, in Perthshire, scarcely forty miles from the cathedral city. So now let us travel those forty miles up the Tay valley, past Grandtully with its most unusual old Church of St Mary, past Aberfeldy with its memories of the earliest days of The Black Watch, to Garth, at the foot of the lonely hill road to Rannoch. There the Wolf had one of his lairs. For about twenty years he had owned land in nearby Glenlyon but Garth was part of the Menzies barony until his daughter-in-law Johannete de Meynis let him have it in 1379. There the Wolf built his

castle, on an almost impregnable site, with a ditch guarding its north-west approach and a deep ravine on the other three sides. Sometimes the royal prince was called Cuilean Curta, because he was the King's "excommunicated puppy", his "accursed whelp"; and so Garth Castle became the notorious Caisteal a' Cuilean Curta.

After his death it became respectable again. For a century his descendants lived more or less peacefully there, until another came as wild as himself—Niall Gointe Stewart. This Niall the Doomed became laird in 1499 and within three years, in most unneighbourly fashion, he had burned Weem Castle, the home of the chief of Clan Menzies, whose lands marched with his own. But Niall's worst misdeed came many years later. On 16th August 1545 his second wife Mariota had an accident deep in the ravine beneath the castle walls. The curate of Fortingall was not quite sure what to make of it. He wrote in his diary that she "died or was killed" when a certain Alexander Stewart negligently struck her a blow with a stone in the burn below the castle. Tradition is more

A steep narrow stair within the ancient wall of Garth Castle leads up to the main hall with its modern glass door and its no less modern balcony above.

sure of what happened. It says the deed was planned by Niall Gointe and for his crime he spent the next nine years imprisoned in his own dungeon. From then on, after nightfall, country folk kept well away from Garth Castle. It was haunted. Long ago it fell into ruins but it was partly rebuilt by Sir Donald Currie towards the end of last century and the work was completed in recent times by the late Mr David Fry. Internally it is now one of the most intriguingly untraditional castles in Scotland. A narrow stair in the wall rises dizzily from the outer door to the great hall above the barrel-vaulted cellars. And a "great hall" it certainly is, for it occupies all the rest of the building up to the roof with its large perspex rooflight. Halfway up, where once there was another floor, now there is a balcony with two beds enclosed in tents, tucked into window recesses, and a two-tier bunk for the children occupying what used to be a fireplace. If the children weary of their bunks, they can climb up a rung ladder inside

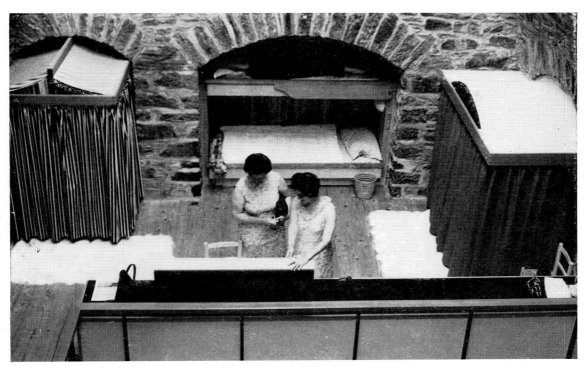

A balcony overlooking the great hall of Garth Castle contains the main bedroom, with canopy beds in window recesses and bunk beds for the children.

The Fortingall yew, the oldest tree in Europe, has part of its trunk enclosed in supporting pillars of stone.

the chimney to another bedroom balcony just under the roof. On warm days you can sun-bathe on the castle roof but the insects are apt to be troublesome with so much greenery around. Over the parapet you can glimpse the sparkle of tumbling water in the burn, 150 feet down at the foot of the den. That was where Mariota Stewart met her death four and a half centuries ago.

Niall was probably buried—like his father, his grandfather and the Wolf himself — in Dunkeld Cathedral. But Mariota the luckless was laid to rest in the shade of an old yew tree in the peaceful little churchyard at Fortingall. She was not the only one who met a violent death and ended up cosily in that lovely spot. There were the two brothers McAllestyr and the seven-year-old son of one of them, all murdered at Stronefernan on the bank of Loch Tay in 1572. The year after that, when Black Donald McEwan was beheaded at Kenmore by command of Sir Colin Campbell of Glenorchy, his head and body were brought to Fortingall for burial. And less than two years later, in January 1576, when three drunk men were killed in a Sunday brawl at Fortingall, they too were buried there. After seven violent deaths in less than three-and-a-half years, peace returned to the village and its churchyard.

It was rather an interesting old yew tree that shaded Mariota's grave. Many a Stewart clansman, in medieval times, went out of his way to cut a branch from it before setting off on some warlike ploy. There was no better wood for a bow. And even then the tree was gnarled with age. Though Garth Castle eventually crumbled into ruins, the yew still lived on. By 1725 its main trunk was fifty-six feet in circumference and no more bows were being cut from it, for bows were out of fashion. But the local tradesmen, the shoemaker and the blacksmith, knew that there they could get the choicest wood to fashion the handle for a tool or a dirk. And each year, when the month of May began, the village boys followed the ancient pagan custom of lighting their Beltane fire at its roots. They did it once too often, for the trunk split apart and the gap widened each year. When Thomas Pennant saw the tree in 1769, people still remembered when the middle part had been united to a height of three feet. Captain Campbell of Glenlyon was one of those who remembered it. Often as a boy he "had climbed over or ridden on the then connecting part." But by the end of that

[20]

About 1725 the main trunk of the Fortingall yew split in two. Within forty years the space between them had already widened so much that you could have driven a coach-and-four through the gap.

The Carn na Marbh still marks the spot where the victims of the Great Plague were buried at Fortingall six centuries ago. In the background, just on the left of the stone, is the Fortingall yew.

On a window ledge behind the pulpit in Fortingall Church is a rare old bell but the one in the niche behind the ornate grille is a thousand years older.

century the two main fragments of the huge trunk were entirely separate. You could have driven a coach-and-four through the middle of the tree.

By that time, people were coming from far and near to see it—and cutting off pieces as souvenirs. But it was showing its years all too plainly. By the middle of last century most of the remaining stem was no more than a shell, thirty-two feet in diameter, with the centre wholly decayed. Drastic measures had to be taken to save it. Some of the surviving parts of the trunk were encased in supporting pillars of stone and a high wall was built around the whole tree, to keep souvenir hunters at bay. Thus, huge and well guarded against its too ardent admirers, the ancient yew tree of Fortingall can be seen to this day in the churchyard alongside the church. And it is still growing. It is the oldest tree in Europe, older than Christianity itself, as old perhaps as its

inscription states: "This ancient world-wide famous tree has stood in this village for many centuries: how many no one can say accurately but from observations made by eminent botanists and those capable of forming an opinion on the matter it seems certain that this specimen of the primeval forest must be well over 3000 years old."

There is another more nebulous tradition about Fortingall, that it was the birthplace of Pontius Pilate. People still find some evidence for that in the Iron Age fort of Dun Geal which overlooks this lovely, strangely English-looking village with its immaculate thatched roofs. The fort, they say, was the residence of King Metellanus and Pilate's birth took place there while his father was on a mission of peace from Caesar Augustus to the Highland King. It is a story, of course, which might be just a little difficult to prove.

There is much more solid evidence of

[23]

another visitor to Fortingall—the Black Plague. In the seventh century it is said to have wiped out every living soul in the village and in the fourteenth century it again scourged the district. In the middle of a field, only a stone's throw from the churchyard, is a standing stone on top of a mound that covers their burying place. An inscription states that the dead were brought there on a sledge, drawn by a white horse that was led by an old woman. They could not be buried in the churchyard, for fear that the plague would start up all over again if their grave was disturbed. Farmers through the centuries have been careful not to plough too close to the Carn na Marbh, the Mound of the Dead. But it has had its moments of excitement, for this was where the Beltane fires were lit each year, after the ceremony at the old yew tree had to be discontinued. It was only in comparatively recent times that the custom was stopped—because the fuel could not be spared.

Two centuries after the plague came, Sir James Macgregor, Dean of Lismore, was the parish priest of Fortingall and his name is familiar to all Gaelic scholars. Before 1512 his brother Duncan and he made a collection of Gaelic songs, the only early one that still survives, and they also wrote a "Chronicle of Fortingall", a record of local happenings. It was in Latin and when they stopped in 1542 the Dean's curate carried it on in a mixture of Latin and very odd English, until 1579.

The Chronicle still survives and so does the church bell which was used by the Dean—and by his predecessors for eight or nine centuries before him. It is one of five ancient Celtic bells which have survived through the ages in Perthshire. There are more in this county than in any other part of Scotland. And, oddly enough, three of the five belonged to churches in this little corner of the county, for besides the one at Fortingall there were two in neighbouring Glenlyon. But we shall come across all five as we go on.

About a century ago the Fortingall bell was moved from the old church to the manse and then it was brought back to the church. Today it lies protected by an ornate grille, in a little niche beside the pulpit. And this is not the only sacred relic in a niche in Highland Perthshire. There was no need, however, to make a niche for another reminder of those early days. No one is likely to run away with the huge seven-sided font just outside the church door.

Having seen all these, we could scarcely have failed to notice something else about Fortingall — the extraordinary number of curiously shaped water-worn stones on top of gateposts everywhere, even on the gateposts of the church itself. We shall come across more of those water-worn stones too, as we continue our journey.

2

Forts of Fionn's Warriors

FORTINGALL IS close to the narrow entrance of Glenlyon and it was in this most Highland of Highland glens that Fionn and his warriors had their forts. The wooded Pass of Lyon forms the entrance to the glen and here the mountains come crowding in so close that at one famous spot, McGregor's Leap, the bed of the valley is only eight yards wide. It is the longest glen in Scotland—thirty-five miles from end to end—and the most overshadowed by high mountains. Towering skywards on the north is Schiehallion, 3547 feet, and even higher and closer on the south is Ben Lawers, 3984 feet. There are farmhouses in the hollow between them that the sun never reaches from mid-October to mid-February, but it is a lovely haven, far from the bustle of the pigmy world.

Though Glenlyon still retains the peace of a hidden valley, it has been more changed by man in the last few years than in all the preceding centuries. Until recently there was a neat little loch, just a mile and a half long, cradled high among the hills at the head of the glen and skirted by a road that ran westwards from Pubil by Tullich and Invermeran. That road has vanished. Today the loch is six miles long, with a massive concrete dam at its eastern end, and the road lies deep beneath its waters. In the side glen of the Conait the hamlet of Lochs and the lochs of Daimh and Giorra were swallowed up in the rising waters of another great reservoir that even more impressively proclaims the works of man.

In the upper reaches of Glenlyon you are apt to find the ancient and the modern jostling each other. Hydro-electric pylons, with their power

A standing stone behind the schoolhouse at Killin marks the reputed grave of Fionn, the great warrior-king.

[26]

Like Fionn's stone at Killin the Bhacain has company now.

lines, stride over the hills and down the glen. There is something slightly incongruous about the sight of them, guarding with their protective arms the ancient Bhacain, round which the glensfolk have woven their legends since time immemorial.

The pylons also straddle Caisteal an Duibhe, the Castle of the Black Hero, one of many old forts that are among the unsolved mysteries of Northern Perthshire. The oddest things happen to those forts. There is one at Loch Tummel with a rowan tree growing in the middle of it, only three hundred yards north of the Queen's View. If you have golfed at Pitlochry, you may have noticed another, when you drove off a tee on top of it. But there are more in Glenlyon than anywhere else. There is one beside a cart road, scarcely half-a-mile west of the farmhouse of Roro. The crofters' children used to learn the Three R's in their school in the middle of it. And, nearby, the United Free Church manse at Camusvrachan rose phoenix-like from the ruins of another — for what builder could resist a site that offered so much dressed stone! The house, no longer a manse, is as pretty as a picture in the summertime, and in its walls you can still recognise some of the stones from the vanished fort. But every pass in Glenlyon — to Rannoch in the north and Loch Tay in the south—was guarded by its fort or its group of forts. Four of them,

close to the roadside, are within a space of little more than a mile, near the end of the public road at Pubil.

No one can say with certainty who built the forts. But tradition associates them with Fionn, the hero King, who kept the peace not only in the Scottish Highlands but in parts of Ireland too, at a time when the Dark Ages were already beginning to envelop the rest of the world. Glenlyon was his legendary home and the forts are said to have been manned by his nine thousand warriors, the Host of the Fians, the flower of Highland chivalry. There is an old Gaelic saying:

> Twelve castles had Fionn
> In the crooked glen of the stones.

To Gaelic speakers the crooked glen of the stones could only mean Glenlyon.

Heroic tales of Fionn's day are part of the folklore of Northern Perthshire and they are by no means confined to Glenlyon. You find them too in Glenshee, Strathearn and Glen Dochart among other places. An old Gaelic poem tells of the death of one of the heroes, the handsome young Diarmid, after a boar hunt among the mountains near the Spittal of Glenshee. Two miles west of Crieff on the road to Comrie is Locherlour. Here, it is said, the swords and armour of the warrior army were fashioned from iron smelted up on the hillside

[27]

When you were strong enough to lift the rounded stone on to the flat one, you had reached manhood and were ready to join Fionn's army.

at Renacardich, the Smith's Sheal. We come across the tradition too, in the little town of Killin at the head of Loch Tay, fourteen miles over the hill road from Glenlyon. Killin is steeped in history and one of its many memorials of the past is a standing stone in a field behind the school, that is said to mark the spot where the mighty Fionn lies buried. He is believed to have died about the end of the Iron Age, in 283 A.D. The standing stone, however, is not all as old as that. People say it was only towards the end of last century that its head was added, when the fallen stone was being re-erected.

Oddly enough, when the mound was opened two centuries ago, no trace of a burial was found. And that was rather surprising, for he was a tall man. Just behind Ardtalnaig, overlooking Loch Tay, two hills stand a mile apart, and they say that one day with a foot on each hill he bent down and drank from the loch. But the stories of Fionn were legion. In olden times, when a traveller arrived for a night's lodging, you could be sure that within the first few minutes his host would be asking the stock question: "A bheil dad agad air an Fhéinn?" — "Can you speak of the days of the Fians?" It was scarcely surprising that the hero king grew with the passing years.

Not everyone believes, however, that Fionn was buried at Killin. Others will tell you he lies deep in the heart of a cave in Skye, with his warriors all around him, in an underground hall so vast that the roof and walls are lost in the depths of the shadows. Once a man intruded and saw them there, a circle of giants with huge shields and spears as large as pine-saplings, and Fionn in the middle, the tallest of them all.

In Glenlyon, anyway, there is tangible evidence of him and his warriors. Close to the fort where the manse was built, at Camus-vrachan, is the Bodach Chraig-Fhiannaidh, a heavy rounded stone, with another flat stone beside it at a slightly higher level. Any youth, it is said, who wanted to join his army, had to be able to lift the rounded stone on to the flat one. There were two similar testing stones in the glen — one at Cashlie and the other at Lochs. They were still being used as a test of manhood long after the days of the Fians. A strapping servant girl had a try one day at Camusvrachan, when the family were away at church. And she covered herself with confusion. The stone rolled back to trap her by her petticoats and there she had to stay a prisoner, until the menfolk coming home from church condescended to release her.

Another traditional link with the warrior king is the Bhacain, on a mound beside the

The hills behind Ardtalnaig, on Lochtayside, remind us that Fionn was a tall man.

The great boulder in Caisteal an Duibhe.

road, far up the glen. Only a stone's throw from one of the forts, it is about two feet high and shaped like the head of a dog. This is said to have been the stake to which the Fians tethered their staghounds with leather thongs, when they returned from the chase. And there were times, no doubt, when Fionn's own dog Bran was among them, with its yellow paws and its black flanks and its chain of pure gold. It was the best hunting dog that ever lived. And there was its brother, the dreaded Grey Hound, that used to roam on its own in the Great Glen, tearing its victims limb from limb, until it too abandoned its wildness and became one of the hounds of the Fians. They say that the dogs' food was thrown to them from the top of Caisteal coin-a-bhacain, the castle of the dogs' stake, upwards of seventy yards to the west. And any dog that failed to catch its supper was turned out of the pack.

Time did not allow the Bhacain to become inanimate like other stones. Even in comparatively recent times it was still regarded with superstitious awe. A retired schoolmaster of Fortingall recorded eighty years ago that it was said to have a mysterious effect on those who crept under its head. And old folk in the glen will tell you that those who did so were

girls. It had become the glen folk's yardstick of virginity. In the late eighteenth century, when the girls returned from gathering the harvest in the ungodly Lowlands, under the stone they went. It was better than all your modern pills.

But of the many reminders of Fionn and his warriors, the most impressive are the ancient circular forts. When they were in use, this peaceful glen must have been a veritable arsenal. One disappeared in a landslide some years ago but the other eleven can still be seen. They had walls as thick as those of an Iron Age broch and like brochs they had only one entrance. But they were much larger. Brochs seldom reach a diameter of forty feet and that is exceptionally small for a circular fort. The one on the golf course at Pitlochry has a diameter of no less than eighty feet inside and 107 feet outside.

Their original height can only be guessed, for little more than the foundations of any now remain. But in the year 1822 one of them was still five feet high and at that time it was thought to be much lower than it once had been. Even today some evidence of their former height still survives. Just beyond the Bhacain and Caisteal coin-a-bhacain, across the road is the best preserved of all the circular forts in Glenlyon, Caisteal an Duibhe, the Castle

Left.—The Bhacain.

[31]

The Iron Age fort of Caisteal an Duibhe

Although the cross commemorates a seventh century saint, the stone itself was probably erected at least a thousand years earlier.

of the Black Hero. It has one unique feature—a great boulder, which happened to be conveniently on the spot and was therefore used by the builders as part of the fort. And this boulder raises an intriguing question. Normally the forts were built with an outer ring and an inner ring, each of drystone masonry, and the middle was filled with rubble. Here the massive boulder, more than twenty feet long and eleven feet thick, became part of the outer ring. And the very odd thing is that the builders still went to the immense trouble of making a complete inner ring, almost eight feet thick, even along the inside of this great boulder. There seems only one possible reason — that the fort was going to be considerably higher than the boulder. And it is ten feet high.

About forty of those circular forts have been found in an area that stretches from Pitlochry to the mountains at the top of Glenlyon and south to Amulree, and all the indications are that they were built by a master race. They may belong to the latter years of the Iron Age or a little later, the beginning of the Dark Ages. Their association with Fionn, in the tales of the Highland bards, makes them the oldest forts in Britain about which a living tradition is still preserved.

But though Glenlyon was so strongly guarded there was one enemy whom not even a master race with all their forts could hold at bay. In 664 A.D. the plague swept over the hills from the south, to leave not a soul alive in Fortingall village. The trail of death rolled up the glen for twelve miles, almost to the hamlet where Eonan the priest lived. He had come from Iona, only a short time before, to settle in busy Glenlyon at Milton Eonan, and in his chapel nearby he set about converting the people from their pagan ways. Then came the plague, up the glen past Invervar and Slatich, until it was scarcely four miles from his chapel. And the glensfolk swarmed around him, clamouring for living proof that the age of miracles was not yet past. So he went down to meet the plague and put his teachings to the test.

At a bend in the road, with vistas far up and down the glen, is a large and strangely impressive rock now known as Chraig-Fhiannaidh — a place once seen not readily forgotten. Eonan climbed on top of this natural pulpit and, with the people on their knees all around him, he prayed that the plague would vanish into a stone a short distance away. And it did. The deep round hole, as neat as if it had been drilled, can be seen to this day. But Eonan had commonsense as well as a flair for miracles. All those who were still in good health were sent off to a mountain shieling, while he stayed behind to tend the sick. And by his miracle or perhaps by his commonsense, from that day on the plague receded.

Although it happened thirteen hundred years

Out of the misty past a stone with a cross, by the roadside at Chraig-Fhiannaidh, marks where Eonan vanquished the plague.

[34]

Beside the cairn on the rock of Chraig-Fhiannaidh people point to the footprint of Glenlyon's saint. But long before his day the Bronze Age folk could have told a very different story about the origin of that footprint.

[35]

ago, the memory of the saint still lingers strong among the glen traditions. Just across the road from the rock, on top of a mound, is Eonan's Cross, rudely carved on a slab of stone to mark the spot where the plague was stopped. And when the rock itself became a place of pilgrimage, people pointed with awe to a carving on top of it. "There," they said, "is the footprint of the saint." But Eonan was not the first to stand there. Some of his sacred relics are a good thousand years older than the saint himself. His cross stone, we can be fairly sure, was a Bronze Age standing stone long before it acquired its unusual cross. And though the plague disappeared into the neat round hole in the other stone, the hole was already there — a cup mark carved in the Bronze Age. As for his footprint, beside the cairn on top of Chraig-Fhiannaidh, there probably you have two cup marks that man or nature has joined together. But Eonan was there and his presence gave them a new and more exciting meaning.

Eonan left the glen after a few years. He became a famous churchman, abbot of Iona, biographer of St Columba and one of the pioneers of Roman Catholicism in Scotland, at a time when the monks of Iona were looking askance at the new-fangled Roman ways. Life on Iona was none too happy for him after that. It is said that he returned to spend his old age in his beloved Glenlyon and that when he died his body was carried in a hammock, down the glen until the ropes snapped, and there he was buried. It was at a little hamlet called Dull, and over his grave there was raised a monastery which later became famous as a seat of learning. Although to the people of Glenlyon Eonan has always been known by that name, elsewhere — and as the biographer of St Columba — he was better known as Adamnan. He wrote nothing about the circular forts, though he must have known far more about them than we do today.

For many a century the district from Chraig-Fhiannaidh up to the Bridge of Balgie and Milton Eonan was the hub of life in the glen. The church was eventually moved from the Milton to Kerrowmore on the other side of the bridge and it was here that one of the great warriors of old, Black John of the Spears, had his home. He seems to have been a McGregor. One of the ancient Gaelic songs in the Dean of Lismore's collection certainly implies that when it describes this "chief of Glenlyon" —

this "king at lifting cattle" — as the "white-toothed falcon of the three glens".

Probably some of these cattle belonged to Clan Chisholm. How he rallied his men at the hill of Kerrowmore and led them to victory against the invading Chisholms is one of the great Highland sagas. Six of his seven sons died in the battle and the outlook was grim indeed, until one of his marksmen shot and killed the Chisholm chief. The place where this chief died, about a mile east of Kerrowmore farmhouse, is still called Clach an t' Siosalaich or Chisholm's Stone. The rest of the invaders turned and fled, and in the rout that followed only the Chisholm piper survived to take news of the disaster back to Strathglass.

Black John was not only a warrior of renown and a king at lifting cattle. He was a good and devout husband too. The church at Kerrowmore was on marshy ground and every time his wife went there her feet got wet. So he built a new church—the church of Brenudh (or St Brandon) about 120 yards away on rising ground. And up to the new church they took an old Celtic bell that had been used for centuries in the church at Kerrowmore—a bell just like the one at Fortingall and so ancient that Eonan himself could have brought it to the glen. It was still at Brenudh Church when Ewen Mc-Condoquhy VcGregor, from Roro, was buried there one January day in 1554 "with a very great lamentation of men and women"—and when Mrs Mald NcAyn Vay, "spous til the clerk McNevin—*God have mercy on her!*—was zirdyt there" in April 1573.

Black John's church fell into ruins long ago but the bell survived. For at least two centuries after the death of Mrs McNevin it lay around the burial ground, unprotected and in no need of protection, for sacrilege was a mortal sin. But Highland faith in human nature began to decline about the end of the eighteenth century, when another of those Perthshire bells was stolen by an English tourist, so a niche with iron bars was built for this one in the graveyard wall. And there it was kept under lock and key until a quarter of a century ago. By that time even a locked niche in an old graveyard was no longer too safe, so a new and more handsome niche was made across the river in the porch of the little white church at Innerwick.

Although very few Celtic bells survive in Scotland, the Brenudh bell is not the only one that existed through the ages in this corner of Glenlyon. Less than three miles farther down at the farm of Balnahanait—the name means a religious settlement—another was found, badly worn, between the wall and eaves of an old cart shed, during alterations in August 1870. Drawings and a description of it were published at the time but all trace of the bell itself has now been lost.

At Innerwick the bell is not the only interesting thing in the church. There is a visitors' book in the porch as well, with a remarkable number of references to the feeling of peace that comes over you there. "A beautiful old church" is one comment ; "a beautiful modern church" is another on the same page. And, in a sense, both are true. Beyond the porch, when you enter the church itself, you see the next surprise—the large stained glass window with its vivid blue of the sky and its purple heather, and the figure of St Andrew with his Scottish cross and his Perthshire catch of salmon. In some parts of Italy St Andrew is in fact the patron saint of fishermen. The window is in memory of Sir Ernest Wills, Bt., who bought Meggernie in 1921. He loved both Scotland and its salmon. In the castle grounds a cairn in the lime tree avenue beside the river marks where he caught his last salmon when he was over eighty.

The rock of Chraig-Fhiannaidh eventually became a motehill, where justice was dispensed. Neighbouring chieftains went there to seal their more binding agreements and on top of the rock there was a famous meeting about 1488. The Fians by that time were only a distant memory and most of the glen was now inhabited by MacIvors, who had come over the hills from Rannoch. It was a disastrous day for them when their chieftain told them to put to death the foster-brother of the Laird of Garth. Stewart of Garth loved this foster-brother like a blood brother and when he heard of the murder he vowed revenge. Seizing his war plaid, red on one side and dark on the other, and rallying his clansmen, he went marching up the glen to Chraig-Fhiannaidh. There he met MacIvor and, while they talked on top of the rock, the Stewart clansmen—in hiding to the east—watched their leader's dark green plaid. But the MacIvors, to the west, were waiting expectantly too.

Suddenly there was a movement among the bushes, close to the rock.

In a niche in the porch of Innerwick
Church is the ancient Brenudh bell.

"What is that?" asked Stewart suspiciously.

"Only a herd of my roes frisking among the rocks," came MacIvor's too casual reply.

"Then it is time for me to call my hounds," cried Stewart, whirling his plaid round to its red side, and at the signal his men leapt to the attack.

The MacIvors were no match for those descendants of the Wolf of Badenoch. With heavy losses they fled far up the glen, only to be cornered again. The Stewarts gained the whole glen by force that day and eventually they became its lawful owners for a time.

Some of the place names still recall that ancient battle. There is Lech-na-cuaran, where each Stewart clansman left a sandal, so that afterwards the survivors would know how many were missing. Ruskich, nearby, was the spot where they unsheathed their swords and Laggan-a-chatha the hollow where the battle was fought. Eight miles farther up is Camus-na-carn, the field of the cairns, where the dead were buried after the MacIvors' last stand. A hundred and fifty of them died that day and

The stained glass window at Innerwick Church.

the old Highland historians, the sennachies, tell us that the river ran so red with their blood that from then on the glen became known as Glenlyon, "the glen of the tinged river." But the sennachies were wrong. The name Glenlyon in fact goes back to much earlier times.

The Stewarts did not long remain owners of the glen. In 1502 it came into the possession of Sir Duncan Campbell of Glenorchy, a man with a flair for acquiring lands. Most of the places named in his charter can be recognised to this day—Gallyn, Meggarne, the Myltoun, Brandvay, Kerochauchy, Cragilk, Crageny [Chraig-Fhiannaidh], Slattich, Laganscassy, Ruskich, Inverbarris, Carnbayne, Inveringlass,

Sestill and Derycammys.

Sir Duncan's son Archibald became the first resident Campbell laird, founder of the family of Campbell of Glenlyon. If we can believe tradition—and Glenlyon abounds in traditions — there were seven McGregor lairds in the glen, one after another, immediately before the Campbells. And this may well have been true, for Roro, where they lived, was not at first part of the lands of Glenlyon.

The first two Campbell lairds lived at Innerwick, until the second of them, Donnachaidh Ruadh na Feileachd (*Red Duncan the Hospitable*), built the castle of Dunan Glas, the ruins of which can still be seen a few

[38]

Carnban Castle became a ruin only a few years after it was built.

miles down the glen. The curate of Fortingall made a note in his Chronicle that on 4th July 1564 "the first stayn was layd in the voltes of the new castell." And soon the castle became famous for a hospitality that was prodigal even by normal Highland standards. It was a well known fact that Red Duncan's generosity was apt to be abused by his less scrupulous visitors. There is the classic story of a wandering bard, who told him such a pitiful tale on a hill path near the castle that he stripped to the skin on the heather track and gave the man his own underwear rather than send him ragged away. And it happened that Red Duncan's wife, looking out of her bedroom window, saw her husband's familiar shape silhouetted against the distant hillside. "Oh, such a large white goose!" she exclaimed. And so the castle ceased to be known as Dunan Glas and became Carnban instead, in memory of her goose.

The kindly Duncan had more sorrow than joy in his life. When his son Colin was born at Innerwick, seven years before Carnban was built, the curate of Fortingall made a note in his Chronicle: "God gif hym grace til be ane gud man and til prospyr veyll in bodi and sawyll." But the prayer was not answered. This son became the notorious Cailean Gorach, Mad Colin Campbell. And there was a daughter who brought sorrow too. She married Gregor McGregor, the ill-fated chief of a landless clan, proscribed and hunted down by command of Parliament. Gregor was arrested at Carnban and carried off to be executed. But Red Duncan was dead by that time. He died in 1578 and was buried beside his kinsmen, the Campbells of Glenorchy, in the Chapel of Finlarig at the head of Loch Tay — "to whose soul," wrote the curate, "may God be gracious. He was not avaricious."

His castle has long been in ruins. A few years after his death a party of Lochaber caterans came over the hills and one of them, from across the river, fired an arrow with a wisp of burning tow into the thatched roof. The whole building was set alight. But the oblong tower with its arched doorway can still be seen in a clump of trees on top of a steep hill that commands a view far up the glen to Invervar. There are trees now even inside the castle hall. And in spite of the white goose it should perhaps be added that the lands around it were already known as Carnbayne when the Campbells first came to the glen.

Here is the strangest of all the strange stories of Glenlyon

3

The Campbells of Meggernie Castle

RED DUNCAN was succeeded by Colin, the most colourful of the Campbells of Glenlyon. He lived in a lawless and a superstitious age. His tenants were pastoral farmers and early each summer they would set off on a journey sometimes of twenty miles and more, with their women and children, their horses, cattle and sheep, their household goods and dairy utensils, up along the shore of Loch Lyon, past Staing Cailliche (*The Old Woman's Pool*), into Glen Meran and on to the shielings where they spent the long summer months. The cattle grew fat on the green grass, manured until it was rich and lush through centuries of use, and down the glen at their winter homestead the crops in the unfenced fields were ripening all the better too for the absence of the cattle. The women took their spinning wheels and the bard his clarsach. For young and old those annual migrations were the happiest time of the year. But you had to take sensible precautions. Before setting off for the shieling you had to remember the Beltane ceremony on the first of May, as your father, your grandfather and his father had done before you. Not that you were likely to forget it! From villages all over Highland Perthshire the cow-herds gathered on the moors in their hundreds, to take part in the ceremony.

Round a mound of turf they dug a trench big enough to take all the company and on the turf in the middle they kindled a wood fire. There they stirred up a custard concocted of eggs, butter, oatmeal and milk. Having poured some on the ground, just to avoid bad luck, they supped the rest, while their oatcakes were toasting on the embers. And these were no ordinary oatcakes. Each had nine lumps like nipples on top and every lump was there for a reason. The cow-herd, with his face to the fire, would break off the first knob. Throwing it over his shoulder, he exclaimed: "This I give to thee. Preserve thou my horses." Then he would break off the next lump and do the same again — "This to thee. Preserve thou my sheep." When he had finished with the livestock he went on to appease the beasts and birds of prey. Over his shoulder went another lump— "This to thee, O Fox! Spare thou my lambs." And another — "This to thee, O hooded Crow!" or "This to thee, O Eagle!"

The ceremony was still not finished. One oatcake had to be broken up into small pieces — enough for each member of the company — and when one piece had been blackened with charcoal they were all put into a bonnet. Then the draw took place, with each of the cow-herds blindfolded as he went forward. The one who drew the blackened piece played the final part in the day's events by jumping three times through the fire.

It was a ceremony which was observed all over the Highlands, as long as people went up to the shielings, but by 1790 it was fast dying out. The minister of Callander at that time, the Rev. Dr James Robertson, had a special interest in old customs. He was convinced that this one went back to pre-Christian times, when the one who drew the blackened piece became a human sacrifice. J. G. Frazer, author of *The Golden Bough*, held the same opinion. But certainly the Protestant cow-herds, in the latter days of the shielings, would have been more than a little surprised to hear such a thing suggested. They thought no more about it than about why they lit two fires that same day and drove their cattle through between. They just did it to chase the devil out of the beasts. It prevented bad luck. That was all.

These precautions, however, were not quite enough, if the migration later that month was up Glenlyon to the fertile grasslands of famed Glen Cailliche, the Old Woman's Glen, that branches west from Glen Meran. It is quite a small glen. From where the Old Woman's Burn rises, fully two thousand feet up in the Old Woman's Marsh between Ben Achaladair and Ben a' Chùirn, on the boundary of Argyllshire, it is scarcely two and a half miles long. But there is magic in it.

In the old days, when folk used the shieling each year, no one had any doubt why it got the name of the Old Woman. Others grew old and died, but she seemed blessed with eternal life. Like the unchanging hills she had been there longer than anyone remembered. People showed something more than just an ordinary respect for her years. At the beginning of May, when the advance party arrived to repair the huts and get the shieling ready for the summer invasion, no one would have dreamt of doing anything else, until first they had thatched her little house, the Taigh-nam-Bodach. And when October arrived and time to leave the shieling for another year, the very last thing they did was to remove the thatch from her roof and carefully seal up every cranny with moss, so that when the icy winds of winter came sweeping down the glen and the snow rose high over the little house, she would be snug and safe inside — with her husband and family.

People were superstitious about the old lady. All through the summer months she sat outside her cottage, like a matriarch with her family around her, and everyone knew that as long as her house was thatched and she was at the door it would be a good summer for everyone at the Glen Cailliche shieling. But it would have been madness not to place the thatching of her cottage first in the list of priorities. When she was displeased, there was nothing but bad weather, bad crops, and disease among the cattle, all through the summer months. It was almost uncanny how it happened.

So each spring and autumn the ritual continued, year after year. When the tenants of Meggernie ceased to use the Cailliche shieling, it was taken over by Chesthill — and a long journey it was — two dozen miles from Chesthill. But still the old lady was there and still her house was thatched each spring and unthatched each autumn. Then the pattern of Highland farming began to change towards the end of the eighteenth century. Blackface sheep were brought from the Southern Uplands to take over the hills and the old happy days of the pastoral life gave way to a loneliness that the landlords found infinitely more rewarding. The cow-herds and the dairymaids could always find a job in the dusty Lowland cotton mills or across the sea in Canada. Thousands of cottages fell into ruins after the big sheep came and even the Cailliche's house had to do without its annual thatching.

Tigh-nam-Bodach.

A slab under this arch in the cellar of Meggernie Castle is said to cover the entrance of an escape tunnel leading down to the river bank.

But she was still there. She is there to this day with her family. They still live in the Taigh-nam-Bodach, though now it is stone roofed instead of thatched. Any summer's day you can see it there, with the white stones that look from a distance like seagulls on top, and you can see the Cailliche herself at the door with her family. She has five children with her at present. Once every hundred years or so, she bears another. Though the baby of the family is still very small, folk are sure it is growing — that one day it will be as big as any of the others. And that is surprising, for they are all of stone, an extraordinarily heavy water-worn stone. They have a weird dumb-bell shape that is said to be found only in one small part of the Cailliche burn. The old lady herself is the biggest of them all. She is about eighteen inches tall and in certain lights you could swear she takes on human features. One of the duties of the shepherd on that beat is to see that the family is still brought out in the late spring and put away again for the winter, and the house carefully sealed up. Odd things, they say, are still happening, when one is foolish enough to tamper with her or her family.

There is no doubt that the Cailliche has been there a long time — so long that even four centuries ago, when first we hear of this glen, it already bore her name. And probably it goes back to pre-Christian times, to the days of the circular forts or even further to the Bronze Age people.

It was not the Cailliche, however, who first brought this little glen into the news in 1583. One June morning that year, a cateran band of sixty men came over the hills at daybreak and into the shieling. Only women were there at the time. The raiders rounded up over eighty cattle, eleven horses and various household goods, and before they left they added black affront by cropping the hair of the Campbell women.

The laird at the time was Colin Campbell, son of Red Duncan the Hospitable, and he did all he could to see that the caterans got their deserts. He ferreted out their names and sent an appeal for justice to the highest court in the land, the Privy Council in Edinburgh. But it was not easy to help a laird so far away and nothing was done. Colin was still smarting from that when by misfortune he got "a clout on the head", and from then on he became unpredictable.

Two years after his trouble with the caterans he moved from Carnban to a new house he had built for himself far up the glen beyond Bridge

[44]

Meggernie Castle.

A stag party
in Glenlyon.

of Balgie. A tower house with a thatched roof, it now forms the west end of Meggernie Castle. And he had scarcely arrived when the caterans struck again. A band from Lochaber came raiding his lands — it may have been the very ones who burned Carnban Castle — and they left two Campbells dead. Colin's son raised all the able-bodied men available and set off in pursuit, and they brought back three dozen cateran captives.

There was no room for them all in the little dungeon under the stair but alongside was the big vaulted cellar with its iron yett and its strong oak door. It was just the size for all of them. One large slab in the south-west corner covers an escape tunnel and some say this was used at times as a handy chute for bodies destined for the river. But if Colin toyed with any thought of despatching them that way he sternly put it aside. Instead he sent his son to Edinburgh to find what iron justice the Privy Council would now dispense. The days dragged past and at last a letter from his son arrived with the incredible news that the Privy Council seemed inclined to let them all go free. It was most unjust. So Colin shot the leader and strung up the rest, each on a separate tree, on

an avenue about a mile east of the castle. The sight of them swinging in the breeze greeted his law-abiding son on his home-coming. The spot is still known as Leachd nan Abrach, the Rock of the Lochaber Men.

Colin survived that indiscretion but a few years later he was involved in another no less sensational. His wife had died just after the castle was built and for two years he lived in sober mourning before starting to look around. Then one day he thought of Agnes Sinclair, the widowed Countess of Errol, a most suitable match for a Highland gentleman. With a hundred of his clansmen he went down to the Lowlands, to Inchtuthil House, and escorted her back in triumph along the hill tracks towards Glenlyon. She swore on her solemn oath he would have raped her, if the Earl of Atholl had not come to her rescue a dozen miles from her home.

The Campbells of Glenlyon were unlucky that way. Another of the lairds had the same frustrating experience when he ran off with Baby Livingston. She too escaped and a ballad was written about her adventures:

> O bonny Baby Livingston
> Went forth to view the hay,
> And by it came him Glenlyon,
> Sta' bonny Baby away.
>
> O first he's ta'en her silken coat,
> And neist her satten gown,
> Syne row'd her in a tartan plaid,
> And hap'd her roun' and roun'.
>
> He has set her upon his steed
> And roundly rode away,
> And ne'er loot her look back again
> The live-long summer's day.
>
> He's carried her o'er hills and muirs
> Till they came to a Highland glen,
> And there he's met his brother John,
> With twenty armèd men.

Old Jock was once a royal stag

Child of
the red deer.

O there were cows, and there were ewes,
    And lasses milking there!
But Baby ne'er ance look'd about,
    Her heart was fill'd wi' care.

Glenlyon took her in his arms,
    And kiss'd her, cheek and chin;
Says, 'I'd gie a' these cows and ewes
    But ae kind look to win.'—

'O ae kind look ye ne'er shall get,
    Nor win a smile frae me,
Unless to me you'll favour shew,
    And take me to Dundee.'—

'Dundee, Baby? Dundee, Baby?
    Dundee you ne'er shall see
Till I've carried you to Glenlyon
    And have my bride made thee.

'We'll stay a while at Auchingour
    And get sweet milk and cheese,
And syne we'll gang to Glenlyon,
    And there live at our ease.'—

'I winna stay at Auchingour,
    Nor eat sweet milk and cheese,
Nor go with thee to Glenlyon,
    For there I'll ne'er find ease.'

Then out it spake his brother John,
    'O were I in your place,
I'd take that lady hame again,
    For a' her bonny face.

'Commend me to the lass that's kind,
    Tho' na so gently born;
And, gin her heart I coudna gain,
    To take her hand I'd scorn.'—

'O haud your tongue now, John,' he says,
    'You wis na what you say;
For I have lo'ed that bonny face
    This twelve month and a day.

'And tho' I've lo'ed her lang and sair,
    A smile I ne'er cou'd win;
Yet what I've got ance in my power
    To keep I think nae sin.'

When they came to Glenlyon Castle,
    They lighted at the yate,
And out it came his sisters three,
    Wha did them kindly greet.

O they've ta'en Baby by the hands
    And led her o'er the green,
And ilka lady spake a word,
    But bonny Baby spake nane.

Then out it spake her bonny Jean,
    The youngest o' the three;
'O lady, dinna look sae sad,
    But tell your grief to me.'—

'O wherefore should I tell my grief,
    Since lax I canna find?
I'm stown frae a' my kin and friends,
    And my love I left behind.

'But had I paper, pen and ink,
    Before that it were day,
I yet might get a letter sent
    In time to Johny Hay.'

O she's got paper, pen and ink,
    And candle that she might see,
And she has written a broad letter
    To Johny at Dundee.

And she has gotten a bonny boy,
    That was baith swift and strang,
Wi' philabeg and bonnet blue,
    Her errand for to gang.

"O there were cows, and there were ewes, and lasses milking there!"

You could never be quite sure whether the lady was really a hind or just a fairy that had changed her shape. It happened so often.

Baby Livingston could have worn this talisman brooch if she had married Glenlyon. It is believed to have been in the possession of the Campbells of Glenlyon for fully four centuries before it was bought by the British Museum in 1897. On the back, for luck, are the names of the three wise men.

'O boy, gin ye'd my blessing win
　　And help me in my need,
Run wi' this letter to my love,
　　And bid him come wi' speed.

'And here's a chain of good red gowd,
　　And gowden guineas three,
And when you've well your errand done,
　　You'll get them for your fee.'

The boy he ran o'er hill and dale,
　　Fast as a bird cou'd flee,
And ere the sun was twa hours height
　　The boy was at Dundee.

And when he came to Johny's door
　　He knocked loud and sair;
Then Johny to the window came,
　　And loudly cry'd, 'Wha's there?' —

'O here's a letter I have brought,
　　Which ye maun quickly read,
And, gin ye wou'd your lady save,
　　Gang back wi' me wi' speed.'

O when he had the letter read,
　　An angry man was he:
He says, 'Glenlyon, thou shalt rue
　　This deed of villany!

'Woe be to thee, Glenlyon!' he says,
　　'An ill death may thou dee!
Thou micht hae ta'en anither woman,
　　And let my lady be.

'O saddle to me the black, the black,
　　O saddle to me the brown,
O saddle to me the swiftest steed
　　That e'er rade frae the town,

'And arm ye well, my merry men a',
　　And follow me to the glen,

For I vow I'll neither eat nor sleep
　　Till I get my love again.'

He's mounted on a milk-white steed,
　　The boy upon a gray,
And they got to Glenlyon's castle
　　About the close of day.

As Baby at her window stood,
　　The west wind saft did bla';
She heard her Johny's well-kent voice
　　Beneath the castle wa'.

'O Baby, haste, the window jump!
　　I'll kep you in my arm;
My merry men a' are at the yate,
　　To rescue you frae harm.'

She's to the window fixt her sheets
　　And slipped safely down,
And Johny catch'd her in his arms,
　　Ne'er loot her touch the ground.

She's mounted on her Johny's horse,
　　Fu' blithely can she say,—
'Glenlyon, you hae lost your bride!
　　She's aff wi' Johny Hay!'

Glenlyon and his brother John
　　Were birling in the ha',
When they heard Johny's bridle ring,
　　As fast he rade awa'.

'Rise, Jock! gang oot and meet the priest,
　　I hear his bridle ring!
My Baby now shall be my wife
　　Before the laverocks sing.'—

'O brother, this is not the priest;
    I fear he'll come owre late;
For armèd men with shining brands
    Stand at the castle-yate.'—

Haste Donald, Duncan, Dugald, Hugh!
    Haste, take your sword and spier!
We'll gar these traytors rue the hour
    That e'er they ventured here.'

The Highland men drew their claymores,
    And gae a warlike shout,
But Johny's merry men kept the yate,
    Nae ane durst venture out.

The lovers rade the live-lang night,
    And safe gat on their way,
And bonny Baby Livingston
    Has gotten Johny Hay.

'Awa', Glenlyon! fy for shame!
    Gae hide ye in some den!
You've latten your bride be stown frae you,
    For a' your armed men.'

Although the lairds of Glenlyon were unlucky, their methods were not altogether
unusual. The caveman method in those days
was deemed as good a way as any of starting
married life. Sir Walter Scott records one
testimonial by an old lady he met. Her mother,
she told him, "had never seen her father till the
night he brought her up from the Lennox, with
ten head of black cattle, and there had not
been a happier couple in the country."

Colin Campbell perhaps would have fared
better if he had aimed less high than the
Countess of Errol. She was really most
annoyed. His love call was sent echoing through
the law courts of Edinburgh before it finally
died away and was forgotten. The glensfolk
by that time were in no doubt that he was
"gorach" and eventually even the Government
was convinced of that. His son was put in
charge of the estate. But usually there was
method in his madness and no lack of com-
panions for his wilder ploys. Once, when the
Earl of Argyll and Lord Ogilvy of Airlie were
at daggers drawn, Colin led a band of his
Campbell men on a foray far down Glenshee,
to bring back a herd of prime fat cattle from
the wealthiest of Lord Ogilvy's tenants. But he
was not always reiving. At times he settled
down happily to enjoy the simple pleasures of
country life. Each summer he went off with his
special friends to the Forest of Mamlorn,
where they built their huts and spent their

time very pleasantly, "schuting and slaying in
grite nowmer the deir and wylde beistis". The
only person who did not altogether enjoy those
happy summer days was his kinsman, Sir
Duncan Campbell, for it was on his estate and
very much against his will that those annual
hunting parties took place. Eventually he
became so annoyed that in 1596 he demanded
powers from the Privy Council to stop this
trespassing. And they agreed that his request
was reasonable—that he should be allowed to
go up to the shieling and destroy the huts. But
Colin had the last laugh. He wasn't needing the
huts any more. The mad Laird of Glenlyon was
dead before the next summer came round.

There were still wolves on the hills around
Glenlyon in those days. Two years before he
died, one of them attacked a two-year-old quey
at the foot of Ben Doran and killed it. But
there is no record of them attacking people,
though folks did say it was safer to bury the
dead on an island.

Half-a-century later, Colin's grandson died in
his prime, leaving a widow who outlived three
husbands at Meggernie. By her Campbell
husband she had an only son Robert, the most
detested man of his day. Her second husband
was Patrick Roy McGregor and by a daughter
of that marriage she became the grandmother
of the most famous of all the McGregors, the
legendary Rob Roy. And by her third marriage
she had a daughter who is also not quite
forgotten. The son of the first marriage and the
daughter of the third saw with their own eyes
the massacre of Glencoe. The girl was married
to a son of Macdonald of Glencoe and after the
massacre she trudged mile after mile through a
snowstorm in search of shelter. Her step-
brother, Captain Robert Campbell, saw it
from a different angle. He was in charge of the
Government troops who carried out the
slaughter.

The Campbells were never a popular clan—
they were too powerful and too successful and
their chiefs were too astute for that — but
it was Captain Campbell who brought them
into disrepute for generations. He disgraced not
only his own family but all who bore his name.
All his life he had been a trial. One of his first
acts of folly was his transformation of
Meggernie Castle into one of the stately homes
of Perthshire. He renewed the tower roof and
put slates on instead of thatch. To this day you
can see his initials and those of his wife with

[52]

Though charred roots are all around, only an occasional tree remains in the valley of the Conait, once one of the most heavily wooded parts of Glenlyon.

the date 1673, on the pediment of one of the windows there. And he added an elegant modern mansion to his ancestor's tower house. But he could not afford such extravagance. Before the workmen had moved out, he was already borrowing money on all sides, even from the tenants on his own and neighbouring estates, in a hopeless bid to meet his overwhelming debts. The McGregors were among the most helpful. Duncan McGregor, corrector of the press at the Savoy, London, gave him a loan. So did another Duncan who had changed his surname to Menzies, and Archibald McGregor who lived over the hills at Ardlarich in Rannoch. Janet McGregor, at Invervar in Glenlyon, gave some of her savings too—and Duncan McGregor, known by that time as Murray, who lived at Roro on the foothills of Ben Lawers. They lent sums varying from 100 to 300 merks. And unlike most of the laird's friends, they patiently waited for as long as thirty years until the Campbell family was able to repay them.

While they waited, they watched the glen being despoiled to satisfy his more persistent creditors. Down came the fir trees that had clothed the hillsides since time immemorial. Above Meggernie Castle, on the banks of the Conait, one wood was two miles square. Farther down was another almost as big, that stretched three miles along the Toiseachd, where the McGregors lived. And there were other fir woods too—in Glen Sassan behind Invervar and over the hill in Glenmore, where the oaks and firs of the ancient Caledonian forest of Osshieschailis stretched five miles along the base of Schiehallion.

The lumberjacks moved into these forests and soon the hills re-echoed to the crash of falling timber. Two thousand logs were sent floating down the Lyon without a thought of how they would reach their destination. They piled up and dammed the river, causing widespread flooding. And over the waters and the hillsides there was the smell of burnt wood, for the workmen set fire to the trees they had left uncut. Local resentment ran high as the old primeval forests gave way to barren hillsides. But it is an ill wind that does no one any good. For generations afterwards the glensfolk used the charred roots for fuel and light—they were better than anything they had ever used before —and there was more than anyone could need. To this day you can still see those roots all around, where the trees once grew.

Not even the sale of the woodlands freed the laird from his creditors. Something still more drastic was needed. His tenants in Glenlyon were far from penniless. They held a meeting and decided to offer him half their cattle to meet his pressing debts, so that the land would still remain in the family. But he turned down the offer and in 1684 he sold almost the entire estate to the Earl of Tullibardine, who later became Duke of Atholl. The only part he could not sell was Chesthill, for it was his mother's jointure land and later his wife's. It became his home, now that he could no longer stay at Meggernie Castle.

He had to live more modestly now but at least he spared his mother the indignity of a quiet funeral. He gave her a memorable send-off. People talked about it for weeks. As a preliminary, to draw the crowd, there were full-scale Highland games, though the pleasure of these was slightly marred when a McGregor of Roro outshone all the Campbells at putting the stone. With a fantastic throw he tossed the stone through the fork of a tree and still sent it farther than any of his rivals.

That night, with the honour of his clan at stake, Captain Campbell sent a messenger far up the glen to summon a shepherd, a giant of a man, who lived fifteen miles away. The shepherd was there by daybreak and as the dawn came creeping over the sky he practised and re-practised the tricky throw. Before the McGregors were out of their beds he was satisfied. Later that morning, without even bothering to take off his cumbersome belted plaid, he sent the stone sailing through the fork to land yards beyond McGregor's. There was a double measure of whisky for everyone, to celebrate that mighty throw, and afterwards the fun was so fast and furious that they had no time to bury her ladyship that day. So they left her till the following morning.

The event which overshadowed all others in the life of Captain Campbell—the Massacre of Glencoe — came a few years later. The Macdonalds of Glencoe were difficult folk. They not only raided the Lowlands with little regard for life and limb, but sometimes for no sensible reason at all they seemed to go out of their way to offend Highland neighbours far more powerful than themselves. There is a stone on the shore of Loch Earn at the entrance to Ardvorlich House, which marks one of their

A thousand logs were sent floating down the Lyon without a thought of how they
would reach their destination.

Glencoe

wilder exploits. A dairymaid at Ardvorlich discovered seven of them armed with firebrands and ready to set the steading alight. She rushed at them and raised such a hulabaloo that the laird came out with his spotted gun — the magic one that kills all foes — and soon every Macdonald was lying dead with the dairymaid unscathed among them. A hole was dug for them down at the roadside, just across the bridge from the east gate, and there they lay until early last century some county council workmen unearthed their mass grave. So a monument was erected to mark the spot and the seven marauding caterans now lie no longer ingloriously forgotten.

A much more serious incident created lasting ill will between the Campbells and the Macdonalds of Glencoe. On 14th June 1646 several of the Campbell aristocracy gathered at Finlarig Castle on the outskirts of Killin to celebrate a christening and the damned Macdonalds chose that day to turn the rejoicings into coronachs. At the height of the festivities a servant brought the incredible news that caterans from Glencoe were deep in the heart of the Breadalbane country and scarcely a mile from the castle, with a great herd of stolen cattle. No permission to bring them through Campbell land had been sought or granted. The scandalised guests, seizing their arms, went streaming out in pursuit. And the Macdonalds, scenting trouble, drove the cattle up to the high ridge above Killin to await the attack.

A colonel sensibly warned the Campbells to avoid the folly of a frontal attack but they ignored his advice and nineteen of them, all Campbells, died that day of arrow wounds. The colonel himself had nine such wounds in his legs and thighs. It was the last time that a Highland clan with bows and arrows came victorious out of an engagement and their triumph was short-lived. An avenging party from Balloch overtook them on the Braes of Glenorchy and inflicted such losses that the Macdonalds gave little trouble in the next few years. But still the whole incident rankled in the memory of the haughty Campbells.

The Campbells were loyal to the Government when Claverhouse raised the Jacobite standard in 1689. But the Macdonalds of Glencoe were in the Jacobite army at the battle of Killiecrankie and on the way home they helped themselves to Campbell cattle from Glenlyon

and Glenorchy. When peace was restored, all the clan chiefs had to take an oath of fidelity to King William — and the laird of Glencoe, independent as ever, was the last to make up his mind. By that time a snowstorm was raging. The final day for taking the oath was past before he took it. And there were politicians in high places who had come to the conclusion by then that it would be a work of charity to root out those Macdonalds of Glencoe — "that damnable sect, the worst in the Highlands."

Campbell of Glenlyon, at that time, was an elderly army officer, stationed in Argyllshire, and in spite of his family tie with Glencoe he was put in command of 120 men and sent to extirpate the Macdonalds. Only one of the men in his party came like himself from Glenlyon. When he reached Glencoe he had little trouble in convincing Macdonald that he had come on a peaceful mission. Quarters were found for his men in the glen and he was made an honoured guest at Inveriggen. There he awaited the final instructions. It was the dead of winter. Most mornings he trudged through the deep snow to visit his step-sister and enjoy a drink with her husband, Glencoe's younger son.

A fortnight passed and then the letter arrived. It was brief and to the point: "You are hereby ordered to fall upon the rebells the Macdonalds of Glenco, and put all to the sword under seventy. You are to have a special care that the old fox and his sons do not escape your hands; you are to secure all the avenues that no man escape."

Captain Campbell put the letter in his pocket and went off to spend the evening playing cards with the laird's two sons. Next day he was to be the guest of the laird at dinner but that was an engagement he would just have to miss. During the night, the laird's elder son was wakened by the noise of preparations and, highly suspicious, he challenged Campbell that mischief was afoot. But the Captain protested he was hardly likely to leave his own step-sister and her husband unwarned if their lives were in danger. And that seemed reasonable. Young Macdonald, with his doubts dispelled, went back to sleep.

It was intended that two hundred clansmen under the age of seventy should die that night. But the plan partly miscarried. A snowstorm delayed four hundred soldiers on their way as reinforcements to help in the slaughter, and they failed to arrive in time to plug the escape holes. The Macdonalds too slept lightly. The attack had scarcely begun when the alarm was up, and more than three out of every four clansmen escaped to the hills in the teeth of the blizzard. No harm would befall them there. If their belted plaid was not already soaked, they would merely dip it in water, wrap themselves in it from head to foot, and lie down in the snow to sleep as snug as at home. But between thirty and forty were dead in the clachan by that time, with a woman, a small boy and Glencoe himself among them.

It was in fact the women and children who had the worst horrors to endure. Stunned by the massacre, they stood helpless while their homes were burned and the cattle driven away. And then, with neither food nor shelter, they trudged off into the blizzard. Somewhere someone would be willing to give them a roof for the night, if they could only keep going. But it was not easy to do that. Most of them—Glencoe's widow among them—died in the snowstorm.

The Macdonalds did not entirely give up their reiving after that but the public outcry which followed the massacre, and lasted for years, put a stop to any more such reprisals by the civilised folk in the south. There was even a chance, after that, of having a death sentence commuted to something slightly more bearable. It happened in the case of one of that clan. Donald McDonald was condemned to death at Perth in December 1701 and on the very day when sentence was passed the Earl of Tullibardine arranged to employ him as a servant. The judge, of course, imposed certain conditions. When the Earl came to collect McDonald he had to bring a metal collar—it could be of brass, iron or copper—to put round the man's neck. And it had to bear the inscription: "Donald McDonald found guilty of death for theft at Perth Decemr. 5, 1701, and gifted as a perpetual servant to John Earl of Tullibardine." The Laird of Glenlyon was dead by that time. A wave of indignation forced the Scottish Parliament to hold an inquiry into the massacre and he was better out of the way at a time like that, so he was hurriedly sent to his regiment in France. There he died in 1695 at the age of sixty-four.

Within a few years a new owner of Meggernie Castle, Archibald Menzies of Culdares, was beginning to reclothe Glenlyon with trees—with the larches and beeches, the limes and elms which help to give the glen its special beauty today. The first larches ever to be grown in Scotland were brought by him from the Tyrol. And he too was responsible for the "arboreal milestones" which marked the distances from Meggernie Castle almost as far as Fortingall — one beech for one mile, four beeches for four, up to eleven for eleven miles. Though two centuries of gales have left their mark, many of those beech trees can still be seen. A great water-worn stone, shaped like a Shetland chair and as large as one, can also be seen standing just outside the door of the tower house at Meggernie Castle. You come across water-worn stones, of one shape or another, wherever you go in this glen.

It would be surprising if Meggernie, in its long and chequered history, had not picked up one or two ghosts of the past. And so we come to the ghost of the lady of Meggernie. They say she was the wife of Captain Robert Menzies, though history does not record that any such captain was laird of Meggernie. You cannot expect more than a glimpse of the lady at any one time, for while part of her haunts the castle there is another part which is only seen down in the little graveyard in the castle park. She was murdered by her jealous husband. He hid her body in a chest, in a closet between two rooms in the old tower which Mad Colin built, and then he shut up the castle and went away for a time to avoid suspicion. Later he returned and, cutting the body in two, crept down to the graveyard at dead of night and buried the one half. Then he returned for the other half — the head, shoulders and arms. But he never finished the job. Next morning he was found dead at the entrance to the tower with a ghastly terrified expression on his face. And so, they say, on dark nights the stump of a body is sometimes seen sitting on a gravestone in the old churchyard and sometimes the rest of her body flits through the bedrooms adjoining the closet. For well over a century people have been seeing her. A laird's wife did so, long ago. A local doctor, in much more modern times, changed his mind and began to believe in ghosts after spending a night in the castle. But the most detailed account was given by two Englishmen who occupied the haunted rooms in 1862. Years later they gave independent statements of what they had seen. Both saw the ghost and both were agreed that a pink light almost as bright as daylight filled their rooms. But that was not all. The first and most vivid recollection of one of them was being wakened in the middle of the night by a searing kiss that felt as if it was scorching the flesh from his cheek-bone. He found it hard to believe that the skin could fail to show signs of burning.

Other strange things have happened too at Meggernie Castle. In the part which Captain Campbell built three centuries ago an addition was made by Ranald Menzies in 1858. He built a chapel upstairs with a stone cross above its dormer window. It became known as the Monk's Room, though there is no evidence that the services held in it were ever Roman Catholic. It is a long time, however, since services of any kind took place there. One day, some years ago, five young people chose that room of all rooms for a seance. It ended less light-heartedly than it began. The voice of the medium trailed to a halt. And then, with a cry "I can't do it!" she collapsed on the floor in a faint. Two of her friends noticed nothing else but the other two are convinced to this day that a sudden smell of incense filled the room. One of them has slept several times in the haunted bedroom and seen no ghost but like many a person who knows Glenlyon well she keeps an open mind on the subject of the supernatural. Looking for logical explanations has never been a specially rewarding pastime in this glen.

A strange thing happened some years ago in this upper room, the Monk's Room, at Meggernie Castle.

Four hundred years ago a chief of Clan Gregor made an almost impossible leap across this gorge in the Pass of Lyon, to escape from pursuing bloodhounds. Since then it has been known as McGregor's Leap.

4

Death
to
Clan
Gregor

ALTHOUGH THE Massacre of Glencoe has gone down in history as the foulest deed ever inflicted on any Highland clan, it was mild compared with what befell Clan Gregor almost a century earlier—and nowhere was their fate more grim than along the shores of Loch Tummel and Loch Rannoch — and over the hills in Glenlyon, the home of two of their most ill-starred chiefs.

Other clans like their neighbours, the Robertsons of Struan, had some lucky charm that kept them safe as long as it was in the chief's possession. But the McGregors had none and no provident angel guarded them in adversity. Eventually they had not even a glen or a name to call their own. They were the landless clan and the nameless clan, bereft of everything but their Highland pride.

It was at the head of Loch Awe in Argyll-shire — around Glenorchy and neighbouring Glenstrae — that the chiefs of the clan had their ancestral home. They were probably of royal race. About the end of the thirteenth century the main line died out in an heiress who married a Campbell. She bore him no children but his descendants became the Campbells of Glenorchy—and they held the superiority of the land from then on, while Clan Gregor continued to occupy it by the power of the sword.

Two centuries later Glenstrae was still the homeland of the clan but two numerous branches had also emerged — the McGregors of Balloch at the foot of Loch Tay and the McGregors of Roro, who lived in the Toiseachd, a six-mile stretch along the south

The nameless gravestones
of forgotten McGregors
almost pave the mound on
which the modern Church
of Glenorchy stands.

bank of the River Lyon, on the foothills of Ben Lawers. At Roro they were probably always outnumbered by the members of other clans. But that was not uncommon. No part of Northern Perthshire seems ever to have been exclusively occupied by any particular clan. One thing, however, is certain. Over a wide area, from the west of Rannoch, sweeping south through Glenlyon and round by Loch Tay and Glen Dochart, no other clan was as numerous as the McGregors. They were settling southwards too, among the MacLarens and Stewarts of Balquhidder and in the country beyond, still closer to the fringe of the Lowlands.

Though the McGregors of Balloch and Roro had their own chieftains, the chief of the clan was McGregor of Glenstrae. His home was Stronmilchan, on the foothills between wild Glenstrae and lovely Glenorchy, and a mile from his mansion was the hamlet we know as Dalmally but they called Dysart. The noblest of the clan were buried for generations beside the high altar in the church at Dysart, and no

matter how far a McGregor might wander from home, there was no peace for his soul unless his body was laid beside those of his ancestors in this Church of Glenorchy at Dysart.

In 1498, when Malcolm McGregor, the chief's eldest son, died in Glenlyon, his kinsmen tramped thirty miles with his body, over peat haggs and heather, to bury him at Dysart in a cist of stones on the south side of the altar. The same thing happened when Black John, the son of Patrick McGregor of Glenstrae, died on Rannochside in 1519. He too was buried in a stone coffin and people long remembered his burial, for that was the day when the giant comet was seen in Glenorchy. A few years later there was another procession of mourners across wild Rannoch moor, when Gregor McGregor died at the Isle of Loch Rannoch. He too was buried "at Dysart, in a cist of stones on the north side of the high altar."

It was only the Glenstrae McGregors, however, who were buried there. The others had their own special places—the Roro line at Brenudh in Glenlyon; the Rannoch ones at Killiechonain, then the largest village on the north shore of Loch Rannoch; the Balloch ones at Inchadin, once the parish church of Kenmore, on the north side of the Tay. There they could rest in peace. But the time was coming when outside the grave there was going to be little peace for any of the clan. Even before 1500 they were beginning to realise, too slowly and too late, that they had been left behind in the rat race of a changing world. It had never mattered, in the old days, whether they owned or the King owned the land where they lived. But now it was different. One after another, the lands where the McGregors lived were passing into the hands of powerful

[62]

Morenish, on Lochtayside, where a McGregor's disloyalty cost him his life.

Five great larch trees mark the spot where McGregor made his famous leap

neighbours and none into the hands of the McGregors. Not even the chief and his leading chieftains had a glen they could call their own.

By 1519 they had lost the power even to choose their own chief. The chieftain of a junior branch — the Clan Dughaill Ciar branch — married a daughter of Campbell of Glenorchy after a whirlwind wooing in which he raped her first, and the bride's father then saw that the real chief of Clan Gregor was disinherited in favour of Glenorchy's new son-in-law. The disinherited line — the Children of the Mist — paid little heed to the law from then on, for it had done them no good. They spent most of their time around Rannoch now, where the wildest and proudest of the clan had their home. It was a land well suited for an independent life. When too much trouble threatened, it was easy to disappear into the Black Wood of Rannoch, where the firs and pines of the Caledonian forest stretched for miles across the hills. Even to this day, in spite of the woodman's axe, it is still the largest surviving part of that oldest of Scottish forests. The Highlanders had a name for anyone who lived there—"Fear so cheann fo'n choille" (*the man whose head is under the wood*). More tersely we would call him an outlaw.

The McGregors lived mainly round the west end of the loch and on both banks of the River Gaur. From the chief of Clan Donnachaidh they legally acquired the lands of Stronefernan on a long-term lease. And across the river at Dunan, where they had lived for many years, they stayed on after the chief of Clan Menzies received it as a gift from the King in 1502. Today the eagle flies over Dunan. In those days the McGregors, with a no less lordly spirit, claimed by the might of the sword that this land belonged to them.

Sir Robert Menzies accepted the fact that the situation was beyond him. In 1523, when the McGregors of Dunan were beginning to feature on a national scale as trouble-makers, the Privy Council ordered him to get them under control. And he replied quite indignantly that the "McGregour on force enterit the said Robertis landis of Rannoche, and withaldis the samyn fra him maisterfullie, and will nocht be put out be him of the saidis landis". So they stayed on unmolested until in 1531 another attempt was made to eject them. This time the King sent the Earl of Atholl to drive them out of their castle on the loch and the Earl succeeded up to

a point. He took the castle and kept them out for several months. But the King was reluctant to pay for a garrison and the Earl had no intention of meeting the cost, so he moved out and the McGregors soon moved back in. They had no real quarrel with him or even with the chief of Clan Menzies. And for many years they settled down to live at peace even with the Campbells of Glenorchy. There was no unfriendliness between them and Sir John Campbell. When he went to Paris in 1537 to attend the wedding of James V and Madeleine de Valois, with him he took Duncan McGregor, the Roro chieftain, with his son Gregor, and Gregor Dougalson, the Balloch chieftain, with his two brothers. Old troubles were so far forgotten that Duncan Ladasach, chieftain of the Children of the Mist and rightful chief of the whole clan, had accepted the role of tutor to the actual chief, young Gregor McGregor.

But the Golden Age came to a sudden end, in the year 1550, when Sir John Campbell of Glenorchy was succeeded by his brother Colin, the Grey Laird. Sir John was only five days dead when the McGregor tenant of Morenish, near the head of Loch Tay, transferred his loyalty from his McGregor chief to this Sir Colin Campbell. There was a clause in the agreement that, if a feud ever arose between Sir Colin and the chief of Clan Gregor, the tenant of Morenish would remain neutral. But that was not enough to leave honour satisfied. A few months later, on a November night, Duncan Ladasach and one of his sons paid a visit to Morenish and put the traitor to death.

Two years later Sir Colin rubbed salt in the McGregor wounds by evicting the aged Balloch chieftain, Gregor Dougalson, from his ancestral home, so that he himself could build a new castle at Balloch. Gregor lived only three years after his eviction and "a great congregation of people" attended his funeral. Duncan Ladasach was dead by that time too. A few months earlier Sir Colin had held out the hand of friendship to Duncan and invited him to Finlarig Castle as his guest. And, having got him there, with two of his sons, he had them hauled to the pit under the castle windows and there they were beheaded.

After that a new guardian had to be found for young Gregor McGregor and Sir Colin chose his own kinsman, Red Duncan Campbell of Glenlyon. The young chief grew up at Carnban Castle, and there he fell in love with

Red Duncan's daughter and married her. Better times at last seemed to be coming. But when Gregor came of age and asked Sir Colin for the tenancy of Glenstrae, where the chiefs of his clan had lived since time immemorial, he got a flat refusal—and the trouble flared up all over again. It spread right through the clan. Gregor himself was soon an outlaw with a long list of crimes to his name and Sir Colin in relentless pursuit.

Once, when Gregor was visiting his wife at Carnban Castle, a band of Sir Colin's men arrived with bloodhounds and pursued him three miles down the glen. Reaching the narrow Pass of Lyon he scrambled down the almost precipitous slope at the narrowest part of the river and made a dizzy leap across the gorge to escape. People still talk about that jump and argue how he did it, and after four centuries the place is still known as McGregor's Leap. Five great larch trees at the roadside, one on the north side and four on the south, now mark the spot. But there were no larches in Scotland when he leapt across. And only one man ever tried to emulate his feat. That one died in the attempt.

In 1569, when McGregor was again at Carnban Castle, his pursuers finally overtook him. Bursting in, they dragged him from bed to prison in Balloch Castle, the ancestral home so recently of his own chieftains. He was kept there for only a few months and then it was recorded of Sir Colin—"besydis that he causit executt to the death mony notable lymmaris, he beheidit the Laird of McGregour himself at Kenmoir in presence of the Erle of Atholl the justice clerk and sundrie other nobillmen."

One of the most poignant of Gaelic elegies is the lament of Gregor's widow Marion, the daughter of Red Duncan Campbell of Glenlyon:

Had my Gregor of his clansmen
    Twelve good men and brave,
I would not now be shedding tears;
    His kin my babe would save.

Ochain, ochain, ochain darling,
    Sad at heart am I;
Ochain, ochain, ochain darling,
    Father hears not our cry.

On oaken block they laid his head,
    And made his blood to flow;
Had I there a cup to hold it,
    I'd sip of it, I know.

Ochain, ochain . . .

O that Finlarig were blazing
    And Balloch burning low,
And that I round my Gregor fair
    My arms could fondly throw.

Ochain, ochain . . .

Though snow and howling tempests
    Should blow, and every storm,
A shelter Gregor would provide
    To shiel my shivering form.

Ba hu, ba hu, my little babe,
    Thou art but tender still;
Thy father's place I greatly fear
    That thou shalt never fill.

The "little babe" was Allaster Roy, the elder of Gregor's two sons. He was then scarcely two years old. As he grew up at Carnban Castle, his skill as a hunter and archer won him the title of "The Arrow of Glenlyon". But all through his youth the clouds were gathering, as rumours came over the hills of the wild deeds of his Rannoch clansmen. As time went on, the disorder spread far beyond the bounds of Rannoch. He was twenty when the simmering trouble suddenly boiled over. Some McGregors in Balquhidder were caught red-handed poaching deer in the royal forest of Glenartney and John Drummond, the keeper, in a moment of folly, decided not to hold them for trial. Instead he cut off their ears and sent them home with murder in their hearts. The Privy Council, well aware that this could scarcely go unavenged, made the Earl of Huntly give his bond that no harm would come to Drummond. The ink on the bond was scarcely dry when the forester was sent out to get venison for the wedding celebrations of James VI and his bride, Princess Anne of Denmark, and that was the last time his family saw him alive. A few hours later his headless body was found on the hillside. The wedding feast had to do without the venison from Glenartney.

It is said that Drummond's married daughter, Mrs Stewart of Ardvorlich, was the first to discover the tragedy — that some McGregors arrived at her door, one of them carrying a parcel wrapped in a plaid, and they asked her for food. She invited them in, gave them oatcakes and cheese, then left them for a few minutes. When she returned, her father's head was propped up in the middle of the table, its mouth stuffed full of the food she had given them. With a shriek she fled insane to the hills

A grim ceremony in the pre-Reformation church at Balquhidder was one of the main causes of the massacre of Clan Gregor.

and there she gave birth to a son who was to be as wild as any McGregor.

When Drummond's death was reported to the young McGregor chief, in Glenlyon, he called an assembly of the whole clan and, with a nice disregard for propriety, he made the meeting place not in the heart of the McGregor country but near where the murder itself took place, at the parish church of Balquhidder, in the land of the MacLarens and the Stewarts of Ardvorlich. For him and his kinsmen at Roro and Rannoch, it meant a long journey over the hills in the dead of winter, but they were there at the appointed time on the following Sunday. Whether the Presbyterian minister of Balquhidder came down from his manse beside the church to join in the ceremony is not recorded. But he can scarcely have been unaware that something unusual was afoot.

The ceremony was impressive. Without a dissenting voice the clansmen agreed that the death of the forester was not just a personal matter concerning only one or two of them but a sentence of doom in which they were all equally involved. The forester's head was there and in token of their solemn decision each man in turn stepped forward to lay his hand on it, while he solemnly swore by all he held sacred that he would defend the executioners with his life. Then they went their several ways home.

The Privy Council heard of it a few days later and were far from pleased. Though they seem to have known nothing about the visit to Ardvorlich, if it ever took place, still they agreed that what they did know was "ethnic and barbarus" and "in maist proude contempt of oure Soverane Lord and his authoritie, and an evil example to utheris wicked lymmaris to do the like." And the King was no less annoyed. It was unforgiveable that even in his wedding celebrations he had not been allowed to forget those accursed McGregors.

The Privy Council drew up a list of 140 of the clansmen who were to be hunted down and brought to trial, and at least one in every seven definitely lived in Glenlyon or Rannoch, while many others on the list may have done so. They included Gregor McIlchallum and his two sons Duncan and William, from Glenlyon; Duncan McConochy Clerach, Allaster McEune and Gregor McConochy with his brother John, from Roro; and, among those from Rannoch, John Dow McConnoquhy Vic Allaster and his brothers Donald and Archibald, John Mc-

Connoquhy VcEan Duy, Malcolm McGregor VcNeill, Challum VcGregor and his brother Duncan McWilliam, Allaster McNeis, Malcolm Glash and his brothers Gregor Ger and John McNeill, and their nephew Gregor Bane.

Eighteen Highland landowners were appointed by the Privy Council to get the 140 dead or alive—and there could have been no escape if those eighteen had been diligent, for it was on their lands that the McGregors lived. But after five months the hunt was still making little progress. Those McGregors who were actually driven from their homes joined forces with other outlaws and, in great companies, hit back along the Lowland fringe. The burnings, slayings and reivings of cattle became so widespread that even barons and gentlemen abandoned their houses and fled. It had gone so far, stormed the irate King, that "thair wer nayther God nor man to comptroll and repres" the contempt and insolence those McGregors were showing. Sir Colin Campbell of Glenorchy was dead by that time but his son, the no less ruthless Sir Duncan, was ordered to pursue them with fire and sword.

By the following month the hunt had reached North Perthshire but it was still not going according to plan. When Campbell's kinsman, the Laird of Lawers, tried to round up the usually law-abiding McGregors of Roro, four men and a boy of the Campbell clan were left dead on the heather and some choice Campbell cattle disappeared with the escaping fugitives.

A few days later, a dozen miles to the north, a band of picked men tried a sudden attack on the McGregors at Stronefernan in Rannoch. But here too the McGregors were forewarned. The Campbells were still miles away, when John Dow McGregor set off with the menfolk, their wives and children, their goods and cattle, over the hills to Blair Castle, thirty miles away. They reached its friendly shelter and the Earl of Atholl gladly opened its gates to them. The local gentry too showed a neighbourly spirit by buckling on their armour and helping the twenty-three McGregor men to send the Campbells fleeing home. Such friendliness would have been surprising if all the official accounts of the misdeeds of the McGregors of Rannoch were true. But this was the last time that the gentlemen of Perthshire were able to show so much kindness.

Events gradually took a more ominous turn. Archibald, Earl of Argyll, was given the task

Four centuries ago few places in Scotland were as notorious as Dunan in Rannoch, the home of the Children of the Mist, the wildest of Clan Gregor.

of bringing the clan finally to heel—and he was as cunning as a fox. For the next year or two he had the McGregors ravaging the lands of his personal enemies. One of these was the Roman Catholic Lord Ogilvy of Airlie, whose Highland estate stretched from the Braes of Angus to the boundaries of Perthshire and Aberdeenshire. Two hundred men, mostly from Clan Gregor, were sent over the hills into Glenisla to rob Lord Ogilvy's tenants of a hundred horses and countless cattle. In June 1602 Allaster and his brother led another raid, in broad daylight, against another of Argyll's enemies, Alexander Colquhoun of Luss, when 108 "great ky" and 28 ordinary ones were lifted from six farms. And then, in February 1603, came the unforgiveable sin. A couple of packmen from Dunan, in Rannoch, had been selling their wares along the Lowland border and they stopped one day to ask for food at Luss, on the estate of Sir Humphrey Colquhoun, another enemy of the Earl of Argyll. To refuse a request for food was almost unheard of in the Highlands, but this time they were refused—and so rudely that they decided to fend for themselves. Up at a shieling on Sir Humphrey's estate they slaughtered a fat wedder and made a meal of it, then continued on their way. Any ordinary sheep would not have been missed for weeks, but they had

chosen the only one with a black tail and a white body — and the hunt was on at once. Within hours they were captured and put to death.

Allaster McGregor maintained for the rest of his life that the Earl of Argyll goaded him into what followed. With four hundred men, he marched south into Dunbartonshire and along the bank of Loch Lomond until he reached the Colquhoun marches. There he sent word to Sir Humphrey that a personal apology and a blood payment to the packmen's relatives would see honour satisfied. But Sir Humphrey was in no mood to bargain. His own clansmen had been reinforced by neighbouring Buchanans and townsmen from Dumbarton. He had no fear of the outcome until the McGregors attacked, and then it was too late.

One of the giants of the battle was Dugald Gar Mor McGregor — a gentle soul whom the chief put in charge of some divinity students, who had come up from Dumbarton to see the fun. No trouble was spared to ensure their safety. Dugald was sent away up the hillside with them, to watch from afar the battle raging below. But still the unforeseen happened. For well over three hundred years, Dugald has been lying peacefully in Fortingall churchyard, but none of the students lived as long as he did. In the heady excitement of the battle, as he

On the banks of Loch Tay.

watched the massacre down below, his right hand gripped his sword and his left hand his dirk, and in a wild upsurge of enthusiasm he slaughtered the lot. That, anyway, is what some of the enemies of the McGregors said. Others were just as sure it was the Laird of Luss and not the Gregor chief they approached — that the laird put them in a barn for safety and there they were found by the McGregors and slaughtered in the general redding-up after the battle. There is, of course, a third version — there is not a scrap of real evidence that any students died at all.

The death roll among the Colquhouns was so great, however, that the battle was long remembered as the Slaughter of Glenfruin. Their dead numbered about 140. Many of them were killed after being taken prisoner but that was a common enough custom in those days. The scale of the plunder, however, was not so common. A cloud of dust hung overhead as the McGregors swept back northwards—with 800 sheep and goats, 600 cattle and 200 horses from the farms around Glenfruin. But the fruits

of victory were not altogether sweet. Among the dead was the chief's only brother, Black John McGregor. And he was lucky to be dead. From that day a curse fell on every living man, woman and child who bore the name of McGregor. They became "the one doomed and unpardonable clan in all the Highlands".

Two months after the battle and just before James VI set off for London to become King of England as well as Scotland, Clan Gregor was proscribed utterly, by Act of the Privy Council, and the very use of the name was forbidden under pain of death. A douce Perth merchant and his three sons were among the first to abandon this "unhappie" ancestral name. Within three months they became Johnstons instead of McGregors and they did it at a price. It cost the father 1000 merks, the eldest son 500 and the other two 300 each, and they had to take a solemn oath that henceforth they would have no dealings or communication with anyone called McGregor.

All who took part in the battle, or gave food or shelter to the victors after, were sentenced

[70]

to death. Bloodhounds were used in the search for them and in the next twelve months almost fifty McGregors were hanged in Edinburgh on one or other of these charges. Some were tried for other crimes besides. Duncan McAllaster Vrek, for example, had also stripped the Laird of Struan's crandoche—his mansion—of all its furniture and furnishings, worth £1000, and Donald McClerich had been in a band of reivers who stole nine cattle in Atholl, two years before. And eight years ago, John Ammonoche McGregor had stolen six sheep and gone unpunished. That was not allowed to be forgotten. And there was Malcolm McCoull Clerich. They found that he was guilty not only of sheltering the chief after the battle. There was the further fact that he had been present or near at hand when a servant of my Lord Atholl was killed, some thirty years before. But whether a man committed one crime or a dozen was of no great importance. The only real distinction was that some were hanged on the Castlehill, some at the Market Cross and others at the Boroughmuir.

Allaster McGregor, the chief of the clan and the most wanted man of all, eluded his pursuers for eight months. Then one day in October he went unsuspecting to a banquet given by his kinsman, the Laird of Ardkinglas, and there, at the laird's island home, he was arrested. Five guards were on the boat that took him to the mainland but he slipped from his bonds and with a sudden jerk hurled the nearest guard overboard. Leaping into the water, he swam strongly for the shore, outstripped the boat and disappeared.

Three months later a message reached him from the Earl of Argyll, inviting him to discuss the future of the clan and promising that he would not be arrested. Allaster, with no reason to suspect treachery, was welcomed with every sign of friendliness. Argyll offered to send two gentlemen to England with him, and to follow himself to plead his case to the King in London. "He had no doubt," McGregor recalled later, "bot his majesty wald, at his requeist, pardoun my offence."

So together they travelled to Edinburgh on the first stage of the journey and ten days later, under armed guard, McGregor took the road to London. He got as far as Berwick. And since he was now over the Border, no one could deny that the Earl had kept his word as a gentleman that he would not fail to let McGregor go to England. From Berwick they brought him back to Edinburgh for trial and there, on 20th January 1604, he was condemned to be hanged with four of his clansmen at the market cross. But on second thoughts four seemed a small retinue to hang beside a chief. So they brought out seven more of his kinsmen, who had been a long time in prison as hostages, and hanged them without trial on the gallows beside him. And "himselff, being chieff, he wes hangit his awin hicht aboue the rest of hes freindis." Seven of those friends who died with him were from Roro.

The death of the chief brought no respite for the rest of the clan. The hunt was still on and fifteen months later the Privy Council drew up their plans for the next stage — "the extermination of that wicked, unhappie and infamous race of lawles lymmaris, callit the Macgregour", till they were "alluterlie extirpat and rooted out."

Sir Duncan Campbell of Glenorchy—"Black Duncan of the Cowl" — played a leading part in the hunt and if we can believe *The Black Book of Taymouth* he had some cause to feel annoyed. Like his ancestors he had been enlarging the vast Breadalbane estates — he added Glen Falloch. One day the McGregors swept through this glen with fire and sword, to leave a trail of damage which cost Sir Duncan a hundred thousand merks. He had just built a new castle that cost him only a fraction of that vast sum. Still, he had some satisfaction. He saw to it that eighteen of the more eminent McGregors were hanged in Edinburgh for that offence—not to mention "sundry others hangit thair and in other places, whose names were superfluous to write".

In 1610 the Earl of Argyll took personal control and the bloody days really began. They lasted three years and during all that time those who still bore the name of McGregor were hunted down like vermin. Some were notorious lawbreakers. Others, with no crime, went into hiding because they were afraid to do anything else, with the shadow of the gallows now hanging over the just and the unjust alike.

The Privy Council did produce one safety valve for those who wished to surrender. A free pardon was guaranteed to anyone who gave himself up to the authorities and brought with him the head of another McGregor of at least as high rank as his own. Two or three heads of more humble clansmen could also be bartered

Above McGregors' Cave
was a look-out to which
the only approach was
by a narrow cleft in
the rock face.

for immunity. The women and children were less harshly treated. No woman was hanged for being the wife or widow of a McGregor. She was merely branded on the face with a sizzling key, so that everyone would know for the rest of her life that she belonged to that accursed tribe, and then she was sent to a Lowland reserve, far from her former home. The children too had their Lowland reserves, where they could grow up unmindful of their wretched heritage. And just as a clansman could cheat the gallows by murdering one or more of his friends, the womenfolk could escape the branding iron by betraying a husband or brother. There were not many who did that. The wife of handsome Jain Buidhe Ruadh (*John of the yellow-reddish hair*), tenant of Invervar in Glenlyon, was one of the few.

There was a "sheltering bed" at Invervar, a hollow in the overhanging rock, fourteen feet long, six feet broad and fully four feet high, with a spring of clear water at one end. When life as a farmer became impossible, Jain McGregor went into hiding there, with the knowledge that his pursuers might come within yards of his lair and still suspect nothing. But one day Campbell of Lawers, the most ruthless of the hunters, waylaid McGregor's wife and to escape the branding iron she came out of the sheltering bed at dawn next morning and walked back and forth, once or twice, before rejoining her husband. He had been watching with growing suspicion but she pointed out that no enemy would be in the glen so early in the morning, and that seemed true enough. He turned over to go to sleep again. Luckily for him, his pursuers were clumsy. A faint noise roused him and in a flash he was off to the hills, never to be seen in those parts again.

The McGregors of Rannoch went into hiding too but with less success. Some of them found a hiding place in a rocky outcrop high on a hill overlooking the Tummel, about three miles east of Kinloch Rannoch, on the shoulder of Schiehallion. Known as McGregors' Cave, it was later turned into a summer house that has since fallen into decay. You can still climb the steep cleft in the rocks that leads up to the look-out on top, with its views far to the east, the north and west. But the McGregors were hounded even from that. They scrambled down the precipitous hillside to the bank of the Tummel and two made a despairing bid to escape to the other side. One reached a rock in mid stream. The other got across to the north bank and began to scramble up the rocky face. And there they too were shot dead. The rock can no longer be seen, for hydro-electric schemes have now turned that part of the river into a lake.

This is not the only spot in that lovely district with grim memories of the McGregors. A mile north-west of the Falls of Tummel, near

The McGregors' Cave on the shoulder of Schiehallion was later turned into a summer house.

Fleeing from their cave the McGregors scrambled down the precipitous hillside, only to be massacred on the edge of this lovely spot on the Tummel.

Bonskeid House, at the east end of Loch Tummel, is a cave on top of a precipitous rock in a steep hillside and the only access is a path so narrow that only one person can enter at a time. Here some of the McGregors took shelter at the time of the persecution. Their hiding place was discovered and a surprise attack was made with overwhelming odds. There was no escape. Some climbed into a tree overhanging the precipice and, in a last despairing bid for life, hung from the branches over the cliff. Their pursuers slashed their arms off and sent them spinning down to their death among the boulders far below.

One who died early in those grim years — probably in the massacre on the bank of the Tummel — was John Dow, the head of the Rannoch McGregors. A brother of the Laird of Lawers claimed to have trapped him in an ambush and cut off his head, and he sought the reward he was legally due — a nineteen years' tack of the lands of Stronefernan. But he claimed it in vain. Robertson of Struan would not have him as a tenant on any terms. Nor did John Dow's widow become the tenant. The Privy Council, knowing that Struan would have had to pay £1000 to McGregor, if he had ever wanted the land back from him, decided there was no need to be so particular with the widow. It was only reasonable to Lowland justice "that the relict and bairns of the said Johnne Dow be removed therefrom as personis unworthie to brook ony benefite within his Majesteis kingdome." So the widow and children were ejected without recompense and the lands reverted to the Laird of Struan.

By 1613 the extirpation was almost complete. Scarcely a couple of dozen fugitives still bore the name of McGregor, though the chieftain of the Roro branch was one of them. He had fled north to find refuge with Cluny Gordon and it was not until 1616 that this "Duncan McGregour of Rora changeit his name and took the name of Duncan Gordoun." Most of them had become Campbells.

By 1613 the Earl of Argyll was able to relax from his labours. It had been a profitable time. Vast sums of money had been collected in fines on those who harboured the McGregors. Yet still the harbouring continued, for Highland compassion had revolted against the continued savagery. There were few now who would refuse either food or shelter to a fugitive McGregor. As for the Earl, who had so badly used and abused the luckless clan, perhaps even he felt there had been a surfeit of blood. To the amazement of his friends he turned Roman Catholic in his latter years and lost his estates and titles in consequence. He spent the twilight of his life as a mild old gentleman in London and one nineteenth century writer was tempted to wonder "whether, in those later and more pensive days of his life, spectres of the butchered McGregors of 1610-13 and of their wives with the key-mark branded on their faces ever came to his bedside."

It may be the memory of those terrible years that prompted the owner of Fincastle House, in 1640, to carve over a window that looks south towards Loch Tummel:

> Blissit ar the merciful
> For they schal obtain merce.
> The feir of the Lord
> Abhoreth wikednes.

Today the wheel has turned full circle. A descendant of the rightful Children of the Mist — of Duncan Ladasach — is now chief of the clan. But you can look in vain in Dunan and Roro and Balloch and Glenstrae for memories of Clan Gregor. Glenstrae is now lonely and largely deserted, and no trace remains of the home of the chiefs at Stronmilchan. A new church of Dalmally now stands on the site of the old church of Dysart where the chiefs and their families were buried in their stone cists beside the high altar. There are stones all around with the names of Campbells — and some of these may have been of McGregor ancestry. But Time has erased the inscriptions from the ancient gravestones that almost pave the mound on which the modern church is standing.

Ruined Dunalastair House from the McGregors' Cave

5
The
Magic Stone
of
Clan
Donnachaidh

Clach na Brataich

ALONG THE SHORES of Loch Rannoch and north across the hills to Struan is the ancient home of Clan Donnachaidh, which proudly claims to be Scotland's oldest family. Its members, now with the surname Robertson, trace their lineage back to Donnachaidh Reamhair, who fought for Bruce at Bannockburn, and beyond him to the Celtic Earls of Atholl. They were of the royal line that occupied the throne of Scotland in the eleventh, twelfth and thirteenth centuries. And Clan Donnachaidh claims to be the sole remaining branch of that royal house. Duncan the Stout—Donnachaidh Reamhair—of Atholl was the great-great-great-grandson of the third and last of those Celtic Earls of Atholl. He was also the first of the family to be known as Lord of Rannoch.

To this day there still survives an heirloom handed down by him—one which the chiefs of Clan Donnachaidh have guarded through the centuries as jealously as if it had been a relic of one of the blessed saints, the miraculous Clach na Brataich. There are two versions of how it was found. The better known today is that Duncan got it on the road to Bannockburn. When his men stopped for a night's sleep on the journey south, they hoisted his standard, as the custom was, and next morning as the pole was being drawn from the ground it brought to light a ball of rock crystal, two inches in diameter and compact of magic. The victory at Bannockburn next day is said to have been the first of many glorious engagements in which

[77]

the stone played a notable part.

But that tradition, unfortunately, goes back little more than a century. It would seem almost incredible that a chief of the clan, knowing such a story, would discard it for one of more humble origin. And so we can only conclude that Colonel Alexander Robertson of Struan, the clan chief two centuries ago, had never heard of this Bannockburn version. According to him, Duncan the Stout had imprisoned Macdougal of Lorne in his castle on the Isle of Loch Rannoch, and Macdougal escaped. Duncan and his clansmen set off in pursuit but nightfall overtook them and they camped on the shore of Loch Ericht. It was there, he tells us, that they found the Clach na Brataich, as they were pulling their chief's standard pole out of the ground next morning.

One thing, anyway, is certain. On every momentous occasion since then, no chief would have dreamt of making a decision without first consulting the stone. In wartime, by its changing colour, he could tell whether the outcome was going to be good or bad. But it had peacetime uses too. When epidemics attacked his men or his cattle, they soon recovered after a drink of water into which the chief had dipped the magic ball. It was used as recently as last century for that and a handsome tribute to its powers was recorded in 1799 in a semi-official publication: "Frequent application is made to the present proprietor of this stone, not only by his own tenants, but by people at a great distance, and all of them he has had occasion to examine on the subject seem convinced of its efficacy; insomuch that many of the present generation in Perthshire would think it very strange to hear the thing disputed."

Last century it was still widely believed that, when the stone grew dim or damp, the death of the chief was imminent.

You can no longer see the netted silken pouch which an ancestress of the Marquess of Breadalbane made for it. That has disappeared, like the filigree gold holder which encased it in earlier times. But it still gets around. At the end of last century a chief of the clan took it for safe keeping to the National Museum of Antiquities and there it remained until recently, when Clan Donnachaidh provided themselves with a handsome clan house in the heart of their ancient homeland in Perthshire. Now, each year, the Clach na Brataich winters in the National Museum until about the middle of March. Then spring gets into its blood again. In company with the clan curator, it sets off for its old familiar Highland haunts — for the clan house at Bruar on the Great North Road between Struan and Blair Atholl. You can see it there all through the summer months, until the clan house closes and about mid-October the time returns for another journey back to Edinburgh.

The Clach na Brataich is not the only magic charm stone which has survived through the ages in Highland Perthshire. Another, the Clach Bhuaidh (*Stone of Virtue*), in Glenlyon House at Fortingall, has a reputation for bringing folks back alive from battle. Before the men of Glenlyon set off in 1745 to join Prince Charlie's Jacobite army, they are said to have been given a drink of water in which the stone had been dipped. Only one tailor did not drink it and he alone from the glen was among the dead at Culloden.

The Stewarts of Ardvorlich have a charm stone too, the Clach Dhearg (*Red Stone*), said to have been brought back from one of the Crusades by a fourteenth century ancestor. When cattle turned ill their owners were willing to walk a long way to Ardvorlich for a pail of water in which this stone had been stirred three times sun-wise. The Campbells of Ardeonaig, on the bank of Loch Tay, had another. And there were charm stones earlier than any of these that have not survived. Eonan, in his life of St Columba, tells how at one momentous crisis the saint picked a pebble from the River Ness — one which had the curious property of being able to float in water. The King of the Picts was gravely ill but when he drank from water in which this had been immersed, he was instantly cured. Of the stones which survive, however, the Robertson stone, with its many uses, is by far the most famous of all.

It was Duncan the Stout, the finder of this heirloom, who built the original ancestral home of the chiefs — a fortified house with a garden, that stood on a partly artificial island at the north-west corner of Loch Tummel. The site can still be seen, though it is no longer at the western end of the loch. A hydro-electric scheme raised the level of the waters and now Port-an-eilean (*The Fort of the Island*) is midway along the north bank of a much larger Loch Tummel.

Three wolf heads and a "savage man" in chains, in the armorial bearings of the Robertsons of Struan, recall part of the history of Clan Donnachaidh.

Most of the early legends of the clan are woven around Duncan. He was a noted hunter. For centuries the clansmen talked of the good old days when he used to muster his men above Glen Erochty, just north of Beinn a Chualach between Struan and Loch Rannoch, at a place called Feichovruidh, and with the hounds straining at the leash, off they would go on a wolf hunt. There are still three wolf heads on the armorial bearings of the clan chief and these are said to have been granted to Duncan as a reward for clearing the Atholl forests of wolves. But if he drove them away, they came back. Two-and-a-half centuries later five wolves were among the dead after a great deer hunt that Mary Queen of Scots watched in Atholl.

The next memorable event in the history of the clan came more than a century after Duncan's death. King James I of Scotland was murdered at Perth by Sir Robert Graham and a band of accomplices. Sir Robert fled to the great forest of Osshieschailis, which covered five miles of Glenmore along the southern base of Schiehallion, and here he was eventually tracked down and captured by Robert of Atholl, the chief of Clan Donnachaidh. Out of "favour and love towards this Robert for capturing the dastardly traitor", the new King made him Baron of Struan. His barony comprised the "lands of Strowane, half of Rannach, the lands of Glennerach, the two Bohaspikis, Grannech with its loch and island, Carrie, Innyrcadoune, Farney, Disert, Faskel, Kylheve, Balnegarde and Balnefart, and Glen-

gary with its forest in the earldom of Athole." He also got an addition to his armorial bearings —a "savage man in chains", as a reminder that he caught the wicked Sir Robert Graham.

By capturing the regicide, Robert gained a place alongside Duncan as one of the immortals of the clan. Previously everyone had looked back nostalgically to Duncan — and Robert himself was actually Robert Duncanson of Struan. But, though the clan remained Clan Donnachaidh, all his successors adopted the name of Robertson in honour of this first baron of Struan.

It was not always, of course, that the clansmen specialised in deeds of honour. Less than half-a-century later, Bishop Lauder of Dunkeld found it necessary to imprison one of the clan for cattle stealing. A rescue party invaded the cathedral in the middle of High Mass and the service came to a sudden stop as the bishop ran for his life. At the beginning of the following century too there was a Robertson chief who was "a most potent plunderer". With eight hundred men he ravaged Atholl and the adjoining districts for years before he was finally surprised and killed.

[79]

Near Invervack, the ancient home of the chiefs of Clan Donnachaidh, is old Struan Church. Here the earliest of the chiefs are said to be buried.

The family fortunes were fast declining by that time. A large part of the barony — most of the eastern section including Upper and Lower Bohespie, Glengarry forest, Inverhadden, Trinafour and the Kirkton (or Clachan) of Struan—was sold to the Earl of Atholl in 1515, when he put in an offer too tempting to refuse. "Port-tressit and the Isle of Lochtumel", the ancestral home of the chiefs, was included in the sale. They seem to have lost even their burial place in the church at Struan. In this church was an ancient Celtic bell, of the same type as those in the niches at Fortingall and Innerwick. It was said that bad luck would befall the keepers of this Struan bell if they allowed it to pass into other hands. And now the bell stayed on at Struan with a new keeper. The luck of the Robertsons continued to decline.

Sometimes it is not easy to say where fact ends and fancy begins in the story of Clan Donnachaidh. A Rannoch man is said to have become so jealous of the prosperity that the Struan bell was bringing to the Earl of Atholl and his tenants that he stole across the hills one night to bring the bell to Rannoch. He smuggled it out of the church unseen and reached the top of the hill of Bohespie before he stopped for breath. It was a relief being able to rest the heavy bell for a moment on a stone. But, when he was about to start again, the oblong iron bell refused to budge. As he tugged and tugged, a sudden panic seized him and a frantic urge to get it back to its sanctuary before a curse should fall upon him. And that broke the strange spell. Without any more trouble he was able to take the bell back to the church. Eventually, however, it did leave its ancient home—and in less dramatic fashion. Last century, in spite of its hoary antiquity, it was still being used as the church bell, until a Laird of Lude gave the congregation a new one and took the old one in exchange. Later on, for safer keeping, it was presented to the Perth Museum.

Legend does not say whether it was a Robertson who tried to steal the Struan bell, though certainly by that time they were needing all the luck they could get. Another story of the same period, however, does concern Clan Donnachaidh. North of Loch Rannoch, on the Isle of Dogs on Loch Con, one of the chiefs is said to have built an underground house, where he put his wife. Then off he went to woo the daughter of a McDonald chieftain. When the girl's father asked whether he was already married, he was able to swear like an honest man that no wife of his was above the ground. Duncan the Stout is usually given the credit for that piece of guile, but it is far more likely to have been Iain Reamhair, Ian the Stout, who lived in the early sixteenth century. The wife in the underground house was a daughter of McGregor of Stronefernan and that absolves Duncan, for no McGregors were there until long after he was dead.

When the Robertsons lost their home on Loch Tummel, a fortified manor at Invervack became the chief's main residence. On the south bank of the Garry, it is across the river from the west gates of Blair Castle and near the footbridge. Here, said a writer in 1758, "was the Original House of the Family of Strowan." And it was in this tower house that Robert Robertson of Struan died in 1566. It was said of him that he "was good to those under him, did nothing unjustly, wronged no one. He was a blessing to all his own, and was held in great esteem among his neighbours."

All this time, though the family no longer had the bell of Struan, they still had the magic Clach na Brataich, passed down from each chief to his successor.

Thirteenth and last in the direct line, and in some ways the most notable of all the chiefs of Clan Donnachaidh, was the Jacobite Alexander Robertson of Struan. Born about 1670, he was still a student at St Andrews University when his father's death made him clan chief in November 1688. A few months later—for the first but by no means the last time in his adventurous life—he had to flee the country. Just about the time when he became laird, the Marquis of Claverhouse—"Bonnie Dundee"—began the first of the Jacobite Risings and young Alexander, like many another Highland gentleman, rallied his clansmen to follow the Marquis into battle. Six hundred Robertsons answered the call. But the battle of Killiecrankie had been fought and won — and "Bonnie Dundee" was dead — when the young chief arrived there with his clansmen a day too late.

There were few Highland gentlemen—if any —who could equal one of Alexander's feats, for he took part in all three Jacobite Risings. After the collapse of the first, in 1689, he fled to the Continent and joined the French army. It was not until 1702 that he was allowed to return to

Mount Alexander, built by Col. Alexander Robertson, 15th chief of the clan.

his Perthshire estates. Then he began to build a new house in a lovely spot on a steep mound overlooking the River Tummel and near the site of the present Dunalastair House. At least three houses have stood there at different times. The present one, unoccupied since the war and fast falling into ruin, was built in 1858 after the estate had passed out of the hands of the Robertson chiefs. Before that there was Mount Alexander, built about 1796 by Col. Alexander Robertson, the 15th chief. And the earliest of the three, though probably not the earliest on the site, was the one which the Jacobite 13th chief built. He called his The Hermitage. And that was a rather suitable name for a house where men were always welcome and women never. No woman, as guest or servant, ever crossed its threshold, for he was a lifelong bachelor and a perfervid misogynist. But he liked animals. No creature, it is said, was put to death in the grounds of The Hermitage while he lived there. And he was also a poet of no mean order, with a flair for acid wit. Most of the rooms in his Hermitage had one of his verses above the door. There was even one at the outside gate to set the neighbours' wives talking:

In this small spot whole paradise you'll see,
With all its plants but the forbidden tree.

Here every sort of animal you'll find
Subdued, but woman who betrayed mankind.
All kinds of insects, too, their shelter take
Within these happy groves, except the snake.
In fine, there's nothing poisonous here enclosed,
But all is pure as heaven it first disposed.
Woods, hills and dales with milk and corn abound.
Traveller, pull off thy shoes, 'tis holy ground.

In 1715 his stay at The Hermitage was interrupted when the Earl of Mar raised his standard for the Old Chevalier. Struan took out his Clach na Brataich to find what fortune had in store, and he stared at disaster. A deep internal crack stretched across the heart of the stone. It took more than an evil omen, however, to curb his Jacobite zeal. He was in the middle of the second line with his clansmen at the battle of Sheriffmuir.

Some might say he was perhaps too much of an individualist to be an ideal commander. When the first Highland onslaught sent the English dragoons reeling, Struan is said to have caused some small sensation by rushing out in front of the Jacobite lines, brandishing his purse and shouting to one of the retreating foe: "Turn, caitiff, turn! Fight with me for money, if not for honour."

The collapse of that Rising sent him back to exile in France and this time he rose to the rank of Colonel in the Scots Brigade. In 1725 he

On the hillside overlooking the Tummel, at Dunalastair, is
the vault of the chiefs of Clan Donnachaidh.

was again pardoned and again he resumed his life at The Hermitage.

It is said that, when Bonnie Prince Charlie landed in Scotland and the 'Forty-Five began, the frail old chief went tottering down to Perth to join the Highland army. And the Prince was so touched that "he wept as he embraced the aged chief of Clan Donnachaidh." Struan accompanied the army as far as Prestonpans but he was obviously too old to fight. He was persuaded to return home — in a style befitting such an old warrior, "in Sir John Cope's carriage, and clad in Sir John's fur-lined coat, and wearing his chain, these having been captured amongst the spoil." The record adds: "There was in those days no highway from the post road to Mount Alexander, the chief's house, and after the carriage had been wheeled as far as it could thus be conveyed, it was carried by clansmen the remainder of the way. This carriage was long preserved at Mount Alexander."

There was little happiness for him in his latter years. His lands were confiscated after the last Jacobite Rising and in 1746 Government troops burned his beloved Hermitage. Another of his houses, facing the square in Kinloch Rannoch, went up in flames as well, and so did Carie, on the south shore of Loch Rannoch. Carie was soon rebuilt and here he spent his last years with his sister Margaret. It was an uncomfortable house, "excessive cold, as it never was lined or plastered." The rain came in through the thatched roof and the cattle wandered all over the garden.

The *Scots Magazine* recorded his death on 18th April 1749: "At his house at Carie, in Rannoch, Perthshire, in the 81st year of his age, a bachelor, Alexander Robertson of Struan, chief of his clan." He did not die unmourned. Two thousand people of all ranks are said to have attended his burial in the Struan family vault on the hillside below his Hermitage. Not even Government troops could keep him out of that house of the Struan dead.

There were many who said that his unhappy end was inevitable, with the crack on the Clach na Brataich, and certainly since that day ill fortune has dogged the steps of the chiefs of Clan Donnachaidh. Another Alexander Robertson had the forfeited estates restored to him in 1784 but seventy years later a very large part of them, including Mount Alexander, was sold out of the family. In 1855 a new mansion was built by the chief at Dall, to the west of Carie, but it too had to be sold scarcely six years later. The Barracks, at the west end of Loch Rannoch, was the last remaining part. From 1861 to 1910 it was the home of the chiefs of the clan. But even it was sold in 1926 and all the lands that had once belonged to the Robertsons of Struan had now passed out of their possession — all except a little high-walled enclosure, the vault of the chiefs, that stands in a clump of trees on the hillside at Dunalastair. It contains only one gravestone, erected this century. The others who were laid to rest there have nameless graves. But there is no doubt that this was their vault. As early as 1758 it was described as "a Burying Place which was once a place of Public Worship" and in 1854, when the rest of Dunalastair was sold, it was retained by the chiefs as their burial place. Though the present chief, like his father before him, has spent his whole life in Jamaica, he still owns this Struan vault.

*   *   *

Perhaps one of the attractions of Carie for the 13th chief was the fact that he could disappear into the Black Wood of Rannoch when danger threatened. He was not the only Jacobite lurking as a fugitive in those parts after Culloden. So was many another ex-soldier, including some of the Camerons of Lochaber. And these were not all gentlemen. Within a short time the new inhabitants of Rannoch were acquiring a reputation even worse than that of the McGregors at their angriest, as "the most degenerate and worst principled race in the country."

The Camerons in particular were notorious and none more so than John Du Cameron, who came over in 1745 from France, where he had served as a sergeant in the French Army. A giant of a man, he became known and feared as Sergeant Mor, the undisputed head of a band that operated from the old McGregor lands at Dunan. There is a Gaelic song of those days, *The Shieling Booth of Brae Rannoch*, that crystallises the sergeant's simple philosophy of life:

> Why should we be gearless
> Or of cattle be callow?
> We'll get cows from the Mearns
> And sheep from Glen Gallow.
> On the shielings of Rannoch
> They calm shall be feeding;
> To our cabin so joyful
> The drove we'll be leading.

It was over a wide area that he was doing his reiving, for the Mearns is just south of Aberdeen, while Glen Gallow is still farther away, in the far north of Scotland in Caithness.

Sergeant Mor, however, was not just a cattle thief. He also ran a large-scale insurance scheme for those who wanted protection from other cateran raiders. It operated far into the Lowlands and, though the rates were high, the service was very reliable.

Many a tale was told of his exploits. Once, it was said, on the Lochaber mountains he met an officer from the Fort William garrison and they fell into step together. The officer, a talkative type, confessed that he had lost his way — that he was carrying a large sum of money for the garrison and was praying he would not encounter that murderous robber Sergeant Mor. The unintended insult was too much for the Highlander. In righteous indignation he replied that he was not in the habit of murdering people; that in all his life he had only once shed innocent blood — in Braemar when he was rounding up some cattle —and it had weighed on his conscience ever since. At the time, he added, it upset him so badly that he left the cattle and hurried off with his men, as fast as he could go.

"I take cattle," he explained with dignity. "I don't shed blood." Then, showing the officer how to reach Fort William, he sent him safely on his way with a message to his commanding officer that Sergeant Mor would despise taking gold from a defenceless man who had confided in him.

Like McGregor of Invervar he may have used a sheltering bed when the pursuit became too hot, for there was one in Rannoch on a rocky precipice on the north side of Glen-comrie. Called Leaba Dhannacha Dhuibh-a-mhonaidh (*The Bed of Black Duncan of the Mountain*), it got its name from a Cameron who hid there undetected after Culloden, while soldiers searched and re-searched round the foot of the rock. Sergeant Mor eluded his pursuers for seven years, while he continued his "black mail" and reiving, but in the end an informer brought a party of soldiers, who seized him while he was asleep in a barn at Dunan. For the Braemar affair and the cattle rustling he was executed and suspended from chains at Perth on 23rd November 1753.

A year earlier he had lost one of his more noted henchmen, when Donald Cameron — Donald Bane Leane, as he was often called — was captured and condemned to death for cattle stealing. The authorities decided to make his death an example to the rest, so they

Loch Rannoch and Schiehallion.

brought him back to Kinloch Rannoch and hanged him publicly there. Donald was most annoyed. It was hard, he bitterly complained, to be hanged when he had never committed murder or robbed man or house, or taken anything but cattle off the grass of those with whom he was at feud. But his death served its purpose. It struck terror into the hearts of those who watched and Rannoch was never as troublesome again.

Those inhabitants of Rannoch who were law-abiding must have breathed a sigh of relief when peace eventually came, for it was not just a few outlaws who had been engaged in the black mail syndicate. They ran into hundreds. One person with some knowledge of their activities was the Rev. Duncan McAra, who became parish minister of Fortingall about that time and remained there for over forty years. Rannoch was in his parish and in his old age he recalled what it was like in his youth, when its inhabitants were exacting black mail "from Stirling to Coupar Angus". In the months of September and October, he wrote, they gathered to the number of about 300, built temporary huts, drank whisky all the time, settled accounts for stolen cattle and received balances. Every man then bore arms."

One might ask what they wanted with so much meat. But all over the Highlands the love of it amounted almost to addiction. There was one small band of caterans — probably not more than a dozen — who came down from Deeside and raided some farms on the Lowland fringe at Fern in Angus. They were not even safely back over the hills when they stopped to make a meal of one of the beasts. And that cost them their lives.

For less hurried occasions beef tea — "the broth of sodden flesh" — was a prime favourite and so was blood. Mr McAra records that the men of Rannoch "bled their cows several times in the year, boiled the blood, eat a little of it like bread, and a most lasting meal it was." Down at Fortingall, where people lived a more civilised life, the same thing was happening. He instanced one poor man, with a small farm hard by the manse, who could "by this means, with a boll of meal for every mouth in his family, pass the whole year." A century earlier we hear of the same kind of thing in nearby Kenmore. When food was scarce, there were times when the lord of Breadalbane at his barony court had to impose

penalties on local folk who had been caught bleeding even his lordship's own cattle. It was scarcely surprising that in many a Highland glen when the springtime came the beasts had to be carried out to pasture.

Back in the Middle Ages the diet seems to have been much the same. Jean Froissart refers to the food the Scots took in their Border raids on the English. They could live for a long time, he said, on flesh half-sodden, washed down with a drink of water from a stream. It was only when they had eaten too much flesh that they found it necessary to make oatcakes to warm their stomachs. Alike in the Highlands and Southern Uplands, people in those old days seem to have been compulsive beef-eaters.

They even found—like Rembrandt—a poetic beauty in blood. There is a Gaelic coronach in which the daughter of Mey recalls how handsome her dead lover, the heroic Albin, was:

His teeth were whiter than the fragrant trees,
When blossoms clothe them in the days of
    spring;
A brighter red his glowing cheeks did stain
Than blood of tender heifer newly slain.

No Highlander thought it a crime to go reiving in the Lowland fringe when supplies ran short and the children were hungry. But suddenly after Culloden, with Government troops everywhere, the hazards became enormous. The poet Laird of Struan died only three years after the battle but he saw the change. In one of his last poems he recalled that —

          . . . mountaineers
       (As apt to fight as eat),
Who once could climb the hills like deers,
       Now fainted without meat,
While English hearts, their hunger stanch,
Grew valiant as they crammed their paunch.

In the next few decades the little white-faced sheep round the farmhouse door were to vanish as completely as the caterans. A big-boned coarse-fleeced Blackface breed was coming from the Southern Uplands and bringing many a change. Rough, tough wool was about to replace the soft Highland kind that had for so

Right.—A drink of rain water from the cleft in this stone at East Kindrochit was a well known remedy for whooping cough.

Near the entrance to St Michael's burial ground, on Rannoch-side, is the
Clach nan Ceann, the Stone of the Heads.

long been the housewife's pride. A man could no longer break in a horse for himself when the fancy took him. The thousands of wild horses that roamed the Atholl hills had to go, for the sheep needed all the pasture. A man could no longer spear a salmon or kill a game bird, for the carrying of weapons was forbidden and factors were fussy about what belonged to the absentee landlord. There was no beef tea now. With beef an unattainable luxury, folk had been forced to learn to eat mutton. "The people," wrote the minister of Kilmalie in 1791, "subsist, as may naturally be expected, in a great measure upon the offals of the flock." And so the haggis, that old English dish, finally reached the Highlands.

It was hard to find the rent for the landlord, for there was little work for the men to do in the Highlands and the women with their spinning wheels were being fast driven out of work by the mills in the south. The only really viable export were the children, once they were properly weaned. The Lowland mills could take an endless supply of them — and so, in all too many cases, those Highland children went out of their parents' life forever, in the days before the arrival of the penny post.

But there was less hunger in the glens now, for the potato was being grown and causing a revolution in the Highlanders' diet. After all the uncertainties of the grain crop, it was a godsend. People lived on it for eight or nine months of the year. And for the next half century or so they grew somewhat flabby and notoriously lazy, just as the Red Indians across the Atlantic did, when they too lost their red meat and their traditional way of life.

A new industry arose. People found they could raise the rent by making whisky for the thirsty Lowlanders. But that was soon declared illegal. When they were caught making it unlawfully they were taken to court, where one of the local landlords sat on the bench and fined them, instead of praising them for finding a practical way to meet the ever-increasing rent. They just couldn't win. The drift from the Highlands grew into an avalanche.

*   *   *

But we have wandered away from Rannoch and there is one more tale to tell — one which goes back beyond the Cameron outlaws to the days when people still used bows and arrows, and the McGregors still lived at Dunan. Just west of the Black Wood of Rannoch, midway between the road and the loch, is the old burial ground of St Michael's, with a large rounded stone known as the Clach nan Ceann (*The Stone of the Heads*) at the west side of the entrance.

A very beautiful girl, a McGregor of Dunan, had two admirers—a Cameron of Camghouran and a MacIntosh of Moy. She married Cameron and the unsuccessful lover continued through the years to hate not only her husband but every son she bore. He kept his feelings under control, however, until one St Martin's Day he happened to be in Perth. There he bought some arrows and arranged to collect them later. And when he returned he found that, in his absence, Cameron had arrived and persuaded the shopkeeper to let him have them instead.

MacIntosh was furious. Gathering some friends as hot-headed as himself, he took the road for Camghouran with only one thought in mind — to abduct Mrs Cameron. To his astonishment she refused to go with him. He threatened to brain every one of her children but still she refused. "If you dared," she retorted, "I would not shed a tear."

He seized three of the boys, one after another, and smashed their heads against the Clach nan Ceann before she broke down and agreed to go with him.

That was when her husband arrived with the neighbours. In the ensuing battle MacIntosh and all but one of his accomplices were killed. The one escaped by swimming across the loch and on the far shore a McGregor was waiting to kill him too.

*   *   *

Rannoch, however, was not entirely inhabited by lawless men and tragic women. There were also the fairies. And everyone knew what they did to wee Red Donald, the herd laddie at the Spital above Dalnacardoch. One morning, when his parents wakened in their house at Ardlarich, twelve miles away in Rannoch, they found him sitting at the fireside. He couldn't have come in through the door, for it was still barred as they had left it. He could only have come down the chimney. And that meant the fairies had brought him home. So for the rest of his life he was known to everyone as Red Donald of the Fairies. And there was Ewan the shepherd at the south end of Loch

Ericht. For months they were regular visitors at his lonely cottage. He made them little dishes and wooden spoons and fed them on porridge. But one day, quite unintentionally, he offended a fairy girl and from that day every one of them vanished from his sight. These were just some of the things that happened in Rannoch in the days of the fairies.

It was on the slopes of Schiehallion and at Beinn a Ghlo in Atholl that they mostly lived. in a manner uncommonly like that of ordinary folk. Their women did the cooking and baking, made the butter and ground the meal, spun the wool and wove it into cloth, while their menfolk were as busy as tinkers, "sleeping, dancing and making merry, or sitting round a fire in the middle of the floor." But the fairies, like so much else that was truly Highland, soon began to die out after Culloden.

*   *   *

And now let us retrace our steps over the Hill of Bohespie and down past old Struan Church with its memories of the earliest days of Clan Donnachaidh. Across the bridge beyond the church is a little corner of Atholl that was famous through the centuries for its two healing wells and its whooping cough stone — the district around Invervack, one-time home of the chiefs of Clan Donnachaidh.

Sacred wells are not uncommon in Highland Perthshire. There were scores of them, often but not always with a church or chapel nearby. And there is ample evidence that in many cases they were already sacred before Christianity first arrived in the district — that the early Christian missionaries adopted them as part of their own religion. Eonan makes that abundantly clear in his life of St Columba. He describes how, on a visit to Pictland, the saint heard of a well that "foolish men" worshipped as a god. And very foolish they must have been, for he adds that those who drank from it or washed their hands or feet in it became leprous or blind or, at the least, were stricken by disease or weakness. "The saint," he says, "then blessed the well and from that day the demons departed from the water and not only was it not allowed to injure anyone, but even many diseases among the people were cured by this same well, after it had been blessed and washed in by the saint."

This was no isolated case. The act of blessing was done at so many pagan wells that the Latin words to be used in the ceremony were given in the "Missal of St Columba" for all who might need them: "We humbly beseech you to sanctify the water of this well with your heavenly blessing, for the use of the people, so that, with all temptation by the devil and all pollution removed, whoever drinks from it henceforth may receive in rich measure the blessing of our Lord Jesus Christ."

Through Roman Catholic times and Protestant times the sick continued to be taken to the healing wells almost to within living memory. For many an invalid they were the last hope, at a time when faith healing was the only known cure for so many human ailments.

Those who wanted to be cured, however, had to choose their well carefully. Just any old well wouldn't do. If a mother was worried about her baby's health, she would take it up Loch Tay to Ardtalnaig and on to the once busy hill track that went by Claggan towards Strathearn. About a mile from the shepherd's house at Tomflour was the babies' well and it was still being used a century ago. The Rev. W. A. Gillies, who became minister of Kenmore about 1912, tells of a mother who walked all the way there from Aberfeldy, with her infant child in her arms, some fifty years before that. And "the child", he said, "improved in health after its immersion at the dawn of day in the cold spring".

There were several other specialist wells around Kenmore — one for toothache and another for sore eyes — and in Eastern Perthshire there was one in Kirkmichael parish that worked wonders with scurvy. Yet another, at St Fillans, was excellent for lumbago. If you had bladder trouble, St Serf's Well beside the church at Monivaird was the one for you. Having filled a tub from the well, you plunged your arms in bare to the elbow. And for the relief of gravel or stone in the kidneys the best of all was a spring on the south side of Schiehallion. In the 1830s, people were still travelling ten miles and more to it.

Oddly enough, for measles and whooping cough, people seem seldom if ever to have chosen a well. They would go instead to a stone with a hollow where the rain water gathered and never dried up completely. Right in the middle of a field at Fearnan, on Tayside, is a stone which still bears the name of Clach-na-Gruich (*The Measles Stone*). It is shaped like a chair with a natural hollow in which the rain water gathers and children were still being taken to drink from it in the second half of last century. It is a stone which has been catching the eye for a long time. Cup marks were carved on it in the Bronze Age, but whether it was being used as a healing stone as early as that is a question which no one can answer now.

Measles stones, however, are less common than whooping cough stones. There is one of these in Rannoch, on the hillside north-west of Cuil-Mhor, with a basin hollowed out on top. Another is on the MacNab estate of Kinnell at the top of Loch Tay. And yet another is near Kenmore. Probably the most famous of all, however, is the one scarcely a mile from old Struan Church. What used to be the farmhouse of East Kindrochit stands on the hillside to the south of the road and the stone is about two hundred yards east of this, beside a sheep fank on the edge of a clump of trees. The grey water-worn stone is about 4 ft. 6 in long, 2 ft. 6 in. broad and 2 ft. high, with a deep gash on top, where the water lingers even in long dry spells. When full it holds about half-a-gallon. People were still coming here with their sick children as late as 1860 — and bringing a spoon made from the horn of a living cow. There was no cure without that.

A little farther along the same road were two specialist wells, each for a particular ailment. On the next farm of Pitaldonich (*The Town of the Sunday Burn*) was a well of running water about eighty or ninety yards west of a cottage called Tigh an tobar (*The Well House*). This one was used for treating rheumatic ailments. The story is told of a woman from Fincastle, a martyr to rheumatism for years, who was brought over the hill one day to bathe her legs. She arrived in a wheelbarrow but she walked the four miles home. A little farther on is the other healing well, beyond Invervack, on the west side of a burn about three hundred yards south of the farmhouse of Stewarton and twenty feet above the bed of the burn. It was called Fuaran an chesach, a tribute to its power of curing any kind of fever.

  *   *   *

Just across the River Garry are the policies of Blair Castle, where the Earls and Dukes of Atholl have lived for longer than history can rightly remember. The oldest part of the present building is Cumming's Tower and an early Earl of Atholl was by no means pleased when it was built. He returned from England in 1269 to find that in his absence John Cumming (or Comyn), the lord of Badenoch, had invaded Atholl and started to build this tower for himself. He built a road as well, at a time when roads in the Highlands were almost non-existent. A mid-seventeenth century map-maker records that he made "a way from the yate of Blair in Athoil to Ruffen [Ruthven] in Badenoch . . . for carts to pass with wyne, and the way is called Rad-na-pheny or *way of wane wheills.*" And what better reason could anyone have for making a road than that? But the graceful thought had a gruesome sequel. One day Comyn was thrown from the saddle while riding in Badenoch and his foot was caught in the stirrup. His terrified horse arrived at Blair Castle, dragging along the leg and thigh of this thirsty lord of Badenoch.

The ancient Earls of Atholl lost their title and lands, when they fought against King Robert the Bruce. The title reverted to the Crown and in 1457 it was bestowed on Sir John Stewart, the Queen's half-brother. Until the seventeenth century the Earls of Atholl were Stewarts.

Two of Scotland's most famous deer hunts were held by these Earls. King James V was at one of them with his mother Queen Margaret and the papal ambassador. Specially for them the Earl built a pavilion of wood, three storeys high with a moat all round that was sixteen feet deep and thirty feet wide. The floors were laid out like a garden with flowers. The walls were draped with tapestries and silk arrases. And there was all the food they could possibly want — "ale, beer, wine, both white and claret, malvery, muskadel, Hippocras, aquavitae." They had wheat-bread, main-bread and ginger-bread, as well as meats and game of all kinds including "venison, goose, grice, capon, coney, cran, swan, partridge, plover, duck, drake, brissel-cock and pawnes, black-cock and muir-fowl, cappercaillies." Even the moat was stocked with fish of all kinds including salmon, pike and eels. The King spent three days at the hunting there and people said that it cost the Earl a thousand pounds a day.

This sumptuous palace was built on the River Lochain, on the north side of Beinn a Ghlo, and as soon as the King had gone it was burned to the ground. Traces of its moat could still be seen for centuries afterwards.

In 1563 there was another royal visitor, Mary Queen of Scots. For two months before-hand, almost two thousand Highlanders scoured the woods and mountains as far as

Blair Castle, the last castle in Britain to be besieged.

Badenoch, Mar and Moray in a massive round-up, and on the great day more than a couple of thousand stags, with their hinds and young, came thundering through the valley with the hunters in pursuit. There were huntsmen in Atholl who prided themselves on being able to split a deer in two with one blow of their sword.

It is said that the Queen noticed a wolf in the herd and sent a hound in pursuit, causing a stampede in which two or three of the beaters were trampled to death. But apart from that it was a most successful day. They killed 360 red deer, several roe deer and no less than five wolves altogether.

The last of the Stewart Earls died in 1625 and four years later the title was bestowed on John Murray, Master of Tullibardine, whose mother was heiress of the previous Earl. In 1644 it was at Blair Castle that the Marquis of Montrose launched his great Royalist campaign. In 1652 the castle was captured by Cromwell's troops. In 1715 William Duke of Atholl fought as a Jacobite for the Old Chevalier and lost his lands and title in consequence. His younger brother James became the Duke. And so at the '45 there was the odd position that there were two Dukes of Atholl. The 57-year-old Duke William, a trusted adviser of Prince Charles Edward Stuart, had the honour of unfurling the royal standard at Glenfinnan. Later he was host to the Prince at Blair Castle, while Duke James was following Sir John Cope. Eventually the castle was occupied by Government troops, and Duke William arrived with his Atholl Brigade and besieged it. It was the last castle in Britain to be besieged and this was not forgotten when the Government took stock at the end of the Jacobite Rising. Soon after that, to the profound regret of all who knew and loved the old castle, it was shorn of its strength.

Forty years later the local minister recalled his early memories of it. "I have been upon the top of Blair Castle," he wrote, "when it was quite in the gothic style, three storeys higher than now, and had battlements, with some pieces of cannon upon it. Were it now outwardly in the form it then was, it would probably be upon the whole the greatest curiosity of its kind in Britain." A few years later another writer commented: "I could not suppress a sigh of regret, knowing that the roof had been modernized and that three floors were taken from its height, in place of all the turrets, embrasures, battlements and parapets which prior to the year 1747 made the Castle of Athol the pride and defence of the country, well suited to the rude grandeur of the mountains around it and gave the place such a veritable air of antiquity." In the 1830s people still looked back with regret. The writer of the *New Statistical Account* summed up his feelings: "Whether James, Duke of Atholl, acted from personal feelings or in obedience to a mandate of the privy council, it is much to be regretted that the turrets, embrasures and bartisans of his feudal castle should have been demolished and replaced by a plain pavilion roof."

The Government, however, had reason to feel some concern about the power of those Murrays of Atholl. From discreet enquiries that they made after Culloden, they found that the Duke, if he so desired, could muster 3000 followers, some from as far as Glenalmond and Balquhidder. They were mostly Stewarts of Atholl but there were also five hundred Robertsons who now followed the Duke in preference to the chief of Clan Donnachaidh. And there were "Fergussons, Smalls, Spaldings, Rattrays, Macintoshes in Athole, and Maclarens in Balquhidder, with other broken men in Athole, all followers of the Duke of Atholl." It was scarcely surprising that they felt the time had come to deprive him at least of his fortress.

Outwardly the castle has regained some of its former splendour, for in the peaceful reign of Queen Victoria it was possible to recreate its airy turrets. Inside was always magnificent. Its furniture and furnishings bear the stamp of Scottish history through the centuries, back to when Mary Queen of Scots saw her royal deer hunt and into the still more distant past

Only the silent weeds now visit proud Finlarig Castle

6

On
The Banks
of the
Tay

AS YOU TRAVEL along the road from Aberfeldy, up the Tay valley to Kenmore and Loch Tay, at one point high on the hillside you can look down on Taymouth Castle with its memories of grandeur that has gone. Queen Victoria once stopped her carriage there to brood on happy days that were past. With the Prince Consort she had seen the castle at its most magnificent, but since then the Prince Consort had died and so had her Campbell host, the Marquis of Breadalbane.

This was where Balloch Castle stood in earlier times — Balloch with its memories of the chieftains of Clan Gregor who once lived there. It was in 1473 that the first of the Campbells got a footing in Breadalbane and he got it in exactly the same way as the chief of Clan Donnachaidh got his Barony of Struan — by helping to capture the murderer of King James I. As a reward for that, Sir Colin Campbell of Glenorchy was given the Barony of Lawers, overlooking Loch Tay. By the end of the century he also owned the lands of Balloch, though McGregor chieftains were to continue living there for another half century.

There were not many Campbells around Tayside in those days. Balloch was on the fringe of Stewart and Menzies country. Only about three miles away, young Niall Stewart, the Young Wolf, was reaching manhood at Garth Castle and still nearer were the lands of Sir Robert Menzies of Weem. There were far more McGregors than Campbells, too, around the banks of Loch Tay. At the other end of the loch — in Killin and Glen Dochart — again the

Campbells were far outnumbered by another clan, the MacNabs, whose royal origins went back into the mists of history. The Campbells were still essentially an Argyllshire rather than a Perthshire clan. And so, perhaps wisely, Sir Colin chose an island on Loch Tay for the first Campbell stronghold in this district — Eilean nam Ban Naomh, the Island of Holy Women. A Queen of Scotland lies buried there — Queen Sibylla, wife of King Alexander I. She died in 1122 A.D. while visiting a nunnery on the island. But all trace of her grave and of the nunnery too has long since disappeared. The stones may have been used to build Sir Colin's castle, the ivy-covered ruins of which still rise to a height of about 45 feet.

The people who lived in this district two thousand years before Queen Sibylla have in fact left a much more lasting mark than she did. Only two miles away, beside the farmhouse of Croftmoraig, they built one of the most elaborate stone circles in all Scotland and nearer still the Bronze Age folk spent endless hours carving the innumerable cup marks and cup-and-ring marks on rocks down in the valley and up on the hillsides, reminding us of their presence all along Strath Tay. One of the most elaborate of these stones is the Braes of Balloch boulder near Tombuie Cottage, above Kenmore on the road to Amulree. A further reminder of life in this district in pre-Christian times is the unusual number of sacred wells.

Robert Burns came this way and fell in love with the cliffs and woods, the "outstretching lake", the arches of the bridge "striding o'er the new-born stream." He took a pencil and over the fireplace in the village inn he wrote a poem that can still be seen in what is now the Kenmore Hotel. It closes with the lines:

Here Poesy might wake her heav'n-taught lyre,
And look through Nature with creative fire;
Here, to the wrongs of Fate half reconciled,
Misfortune's lighten'd steps might wander wild;
And Disappointment, in these lonely bounds,
Find balm to soothe her bitter rankling wounds;
Here heart-struck Grief might heav'nward stretch her scan,
And injur'd Worth forget and pardon man.

But it was the Campbells of Glenorchy who made the most lasting impression on this lovely district. One estate after another came into their possession. Sir Colin's successor, Sir Duncan, owned Glenlyon by 1502 and all the lands of Finlarig, in the heart of the

MacNab country, by 1506. Finlarig Castle was scarcely half-a-mile from Ellanryne, the ancestral home for centuries of the chiefs of Clan MacNab. Even what remains of the castle on the Island of Holy Women was probably built by him. In 1509 the servants accidentally set fire to the castle his father had built and in the reconstruction Sir Duncan added a "great hall, chapel and chalmeris". In 1513 he went with his King to Flodden and there he died with the rest of the flower of Scotland's chivalry.

Another Sir Colin Campbell, the ruthlessly ambitious Grey Colin, became Laird of Glenorchy in 1550. Two years later he evicted the McGregor chieftain from Balloch and built a new castle for himself there. It was more convenient than his island home. That same year the MacNab lands at the other end of Loch Tay became his as well. The MacNab of MacNab got a money payment "in his great and known necessity".

If Grey Colin was unpopular, his son, Black Duncan, was much more so. He not only played a leading part in hunting down the McGregors but was also deeply involved in the notorious murder of the Bonnie Earl of Moray. And while he schemed and plotted, he collected still more estates—parts of Atholl and Strathtay, Duneaves and Culdares on the outskirts of Fortingall, Morenish of unhappy memory, even lands as far as Glenfalloch and Menteith. He made large-scale improvements at Finlarig Castle and planted its avenue of lime trees that became known as the Cathedral. Probably it was on his instructions too that the pit was dug, close to the castle windows. There were some ungodly tales of the victims he sent to their death in that pit. The King honoured him by making him a Baronet of Nova Scotia. The Privy Council heard of another side of his character—that he was trafficking with witches and wizards. But that was never entirely proved. And all the time his lands were getting bigger until a large part of Perthshire belonged to him.

So the years rolled on. The Honours of Scotland — the Crown Jewels — were kept at Balloch Castle for two months in 1651, given into Sir Robert Campbell's care to prevent them falling into the hands of Cromwell's English troops. Six weeks later they were used at the coronation of Charles II at Scone and then they disappeared again, to be hidden for years beneath the floor of Kinneff Church in

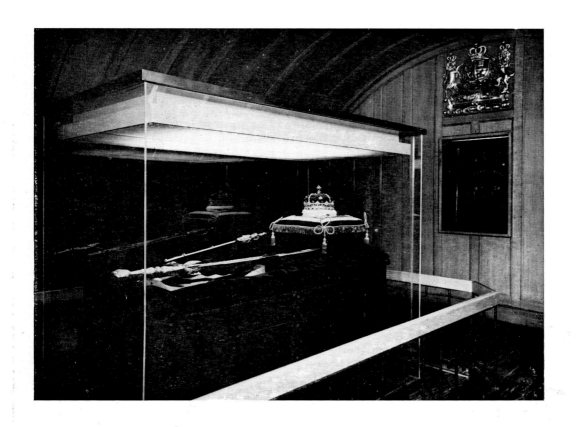

The Honours of Scotland, now safe once more in Edinburgh Castle.

A large stained-glass window in the banqueting hall of Taymouth Castle depicts
the noble line of the Campbells of Breadalbane.

The ceiling above the great staircase at Taymouth Castle is still very much as it was when Queen Victoria saw it in 1842.

the Mearns. By 1654 Balloch Castle itself was occupied by the invading English and so was the castle on the Isle of Loch Tay. The farms were stripped of their crops and such widespread destruction was left that Sir Robert died with his vast estates heavily mortgaged and creditors pressing on every side.

Then came the extrovert Sir John Campbell, who in 1681 was to become the 1st Earl of Breadalbane. At the age of 22, after a whirlwind wooing, he married a London heiress. It is said that two of his Highland ponies were sent specially to London — that he mounted his bride behind him on one and loaded her dowry, all in gold, on the other, and so they jogged north to Balloch with a heavily-armed Highlander trotting on each side of the treasure chest. And who would not provide a bodyguard for ten thousand beautiful golden sovereigns! They helped to bring some of the grandeur back to Balloch Castle but Finlarig with its grim memories of bygone days was left to crumble into ruins at the other end of Loch Tay. Today there are warning notices that those who invade its privacy do so at their own risk. And there is a very real risk from falling stones as you edge your way through the tangled undergrowth in which the castle and the burial chapel of the proud Campbells of

Glenorchy are engulfed side by side.

Well over a century ago one of Sir John's descendants, the 1st Marquis of Breadalbane, demolished Balloch Castle — its name was already changed to Taymouth Castle—and built a magnificent new Taymouth Castle in its place. When the youthful Queen Victoria arrived there with Prince Albert in September 1842, she found it entrancing. This was her first visit to Scotland. Lord Breadalbane's Highlanders, in their Campbell tartan, were drawn up in front of the house. Pipers were playing, guns were firing and crowds cheering. All this and the picturesque dresses and the beauty of the setting made it seem to her one of the finest scenes imaginable. She wrote in her Journal: "It seemed as if a great chieftain in olden feudal times was receiving his sovereign. It was princely and romantic." And then she added: "Lord and Lady Breadalbane took us upstairs, the hall and stairs being lined with Highlanders. The Gothic staircase is of stone and very fine."

They had dinner in the great dining hall with its stained glass windows depicting the long and noble line of those Campbells of Breadalbane, second only in their clan to the Dukes of Argyll. It was the first time anyone had ever dined there. And that night the grounds were illuminated. There were fireworks, and bonfires

Taymouth Castle.

on the hilltops, and in front of the house were Highlanders dancing by torchlight. "I never saw anything so fairy-like," she wrote of the scene. When she left Taymouth Castle three days later, the boatmen were singing Gaelic songs as they rowed her the length of Loch Tay to Auchmore beside Killin.

Many years later she passed that way again and stopped at the point where the road looks down on the castle. "We got out," she wrote, "and looked from this height down upon the house below, the mist having cleared away sufficiently to show us everything; and then, unknown, quite in private, I gazed — not without deep emotion — on the scene of our reception twenty-four years ago, by dear Lord Breadalbane, in a princely style, not to be equalled in grandeur and poetic effect. Albert and I were then only twenty-three, young and happy. How many are gone that were with us then!"

And how many who knew it since then are gone as well! The priceless collection of Old Masters has been taken down from the walls. The furniture and all the lavish furnishings have gone. Even the Civil Defence workers who so recently sat at their little desks in the echoing halls — they too are there no more. Only silence hangs everywhere like the aftermath of a nuclear war. But the halls,

with their imposing fireplaces, their ornate carvings and magnificently painted ceilings, the library with its walls lined to the ceiling with now empty bookshelves, the great dining room with its Gothic stained glass window proudly proclaiming the ancestry of those Campbells of Breadalbane — these still remain.

*   *   *

Five miles down the Tay valley, across the river from Aberfeldy, we come to the heart of the land where the chiefs of Clan Menzies used to live. This was where The Black Watch was born. And centuries before the first of the Menzies family came over from France to settle here — for their clan history goes back only to about the fourteenth century — there was a famous religious community in this corner of Perthshire, while earlier still it was the summer retreat of a saint who made his own bath tub high on the cliff face of steep Weem Rock.

About two miles up the river from Castle Menzies is a village with the curious name of Dull. This was where Eonan was buried when his body was brought down from his home in Glenlyon and soon after that a monastery that became a famous seat of learning was built beside his grave. Its endowments are said to have been transferred to St Andrews University when it was founded.

Though all trace has now disappeared of the monastic buildings at Dull, the massive seven-sided font at the church door doubtless came from it, and a cross which dates back to those far-off days still stands, surrounded by an iron railing, in the middle of the village. An arm of the cross is missing, broken off one day last century, when a horse took fright and the cart it was drawing collided with the stone. There is another reminder of the old monastery in the Scottish National Museum of Antiquities — a carved stone that was found last century while a grave was being dug in the churchyard at Dull. Well over a thousand years old, it gives a glimpse of what those Picts used to wear when they went hunting. They seem to have been a chilly race. There are figures dressed very much the same on a standing stone preserved at St Vigeans on the outskirts of Arbroath. The one at Dull is unusual too in the fact that it is not a standing stone. It seems to have been fastened to a wall.

Close to the present church at Dull is another reminder of those far-off days — Tobar Eonain (*Eonan's Well*), where there were marvellous cures among the faithful.

A mile downstream from the castle is another village no less oddly called Weem. But this word merely comes from the Gaelic *uaim*, meaning "a cave", and there are two caves in the steep, almost precipitous Weem Rock, which towers fully 600 feet behind the castle. The upper one, more a ledge than a cave, had a saint as its occupant, while the lower one was the Devil's. This lower cave, less easy to find than the other, is said by tradition to have extended far through the hill, rising all the time, until about 700 feet higher it came out at the foot of a great rock on the north shore of Loch Glassie, upwards of two miles distant. But only a brave or an avaricious man — or a piper — would have dared to make that journey.

Pipers in the old days had an obsession about caves. They kept marching in, with their bagpipes playing, and gradually the sound grew fainter and fainter, but it never quite disappeared. The piper himself always vanished for ever but the music re-echoed through the years. It happened on the east coast of Scotland in an Angus cave south of Lunan Bay. A piper on his way from a wedding broke his homeward journey to get lost in that cave. It happened in the West Highlands too, in a cave called Uaim-'t' Hoirle, about eight miles up the River Nevis—a cave that was described many years ago as "a frightful habitation of darkness, an abode fit to be inhabited only by the sons of despair." Into it went a piper one day, and he marched until the sound of his pibroch was heard at Kinloch, ten miles away. And when the people heard the lament he was playing—

The Huntsmen of Dull

The sun still casts reflected glory on deserted Castle Menzies

"Oh! that I had three hands, two for the bagpipes and one for the sword!"—they knew he would never come out alive. It happened too at a cave on the shoulder of Schiehallion and at another at Balnagard, even nearer Weem. And though the cave on Weem Rock had no piper, it too was a frightful habitation of darkness, the most frightful of them all.

Inside were nine iron gates, which opened of their own accord in front of you and closed no less mysteriously behind. But that was not altogether exceptional. Only a few miles away — on the south-west foothills of Schiehallion where the Glenmore shielings used to be — you found the same thing at Uamh Tom a' Mhòr-fhir. There too, every few yards, a door opened to let you through, then closed behind you. But the Weem cave was altogether more exciting, for its halls were crammed with treasure worth an emperor's ransom. Even the roofs were studded with precious stones. There was only one slightly awkward feature—that the Devil himself was guarding the treasure. Sometimes he disguised himself as a fierce-eyed monk. Sometimes he was more like a blood-chilling water-kelpie wearing a loose red cloak. It was his water-kelpie outfit that he wore when he murdered the local laird's daughter.

The laird had two daughters, one by his first marriage and the other by his second, and his second wife hated her heiress step-daughter. It was she who arranged that the Devil would entice a heifer into the cave and then the two girls would be sent to play on the hillside. The lowing of the heifer would draw them to the cave and the Devil would easily know which to seize, for her own daughter would be wearing a crucifix or a miniature of the Virgin Mary, or she would be carrying a Bible — there are different versions of the story. But there was one thing she had not foreseen. Just before the girls reached the cave, her daughter took off the talisman and gave it to her sister. So the Devil seized the wrong girl and, slamming the iron gate in the face of the other, carried her off into the darkness. Her mangled body was later found floating on Loch Glassie. An old Gaelic song, *The Song of Weem*, tells the plaintive story:

> Oh! woe on the going
> We went yon day,
> And woe on the lowing
> Brought us this way . . .

People say that until near the end of last century the cave still extended far through the hill and then the local schoolmaster became worried about the safety of his pupils, so he blew up the entrance. Only a few feet remain. But, truth to tell, the rock is not the kind where long underground passages would be expected.

The other cave on Weem Rock is often called St David's Cave, after a Menzies laird who is said to have turned hermit, though certainly he never became officially a saint. The cave's real name is St Cuthbert's Cave. While Eonan was ministering in Glenlyon, about thirteen hundred years ago, there was a young priest called Cuthbert at Melrose Abbey. And he used to wander off, on his own, for months on end, to remote villages "far from the world in wild mountain places and fearful to behold."

The Irish Life of St Cuthbert, a fourteenth century Latin manuscript which claims to come from the ancient histories of the Irish, tells us that his retreat on those occasions was a richly wooded hill a mile from Dull at "Doil-weme": "So, coming to the town which is called Dul, he abandoned city life and chose to be a hermit. Very near to it, not more than a mile distant, in wooded glades, is a very high mountain so steep that it can be approached or climbed only from the south side. This mountain is called Doil-weme by the inhabitants of that region, a name which in Latin means a most beautiful and pleasant area. So, in the darkness of this mountain St Cuthbert began to live alone and before him no one had previously dared to linger there, because of the frequent apparitions of demons."

And the Devil of course in truth was there. He was by no means pleased to have a saint as a neighbour on the ledge above and soon the whole rock was reverberating in a battle of the giants. Cuthbert emerged as victor in that mighty fray and then he set about making his cave more suitable for a hermit's needs. He built an oratory of rough wood and on a stone he made a cross. Then, drawing a spring of water from the solid rock, he carved a bath in a single stone. And many a chilly night he spent, sitting in his bath and praying devoutly until the dawn came up, in the years between 651 and 661 A.D. The same Latin manuscript tells us that one day the daughter of the King of the province accused him of having seduced her. In outraged virtue he

prayed to God, and the earth opened and swallowed up the young woman, so that she was never seen again, not even floating on Loch Glassie. Cuthbert later became Bishop of the great Northumbrian abbey of Lindisfarne. Wrapped in five robes of embroidered silk, he now lies buried in the innermost of three coffins in Durham Cathedral.

For many a century the sick were taken to this cave at Weem to drink from the water of the spring, the Well of the Chapel Craig. It became noted for miraculous cures.

Castle Menzies, now standing empty in the valley below the cave, was the home for centuries of the chiefs of Clan Menzies. They were among the great landowners of Northern Perthshire, with territories which included Dull and Weem in the valley of the Tay, Aberfeldy across the river, and Roro with its shielings many miles away on the north side of Ben Lawers, in the heart of the Campbell country in Glenlyon. They had another large tract too, from the shore of Loch Rannoch to the bounds of Lochaber, far to the north. Menzies of that ilk was a person of some consequence.

Although part of Castle Menzies was built as recently as the 1820s, most of it dates back to 1571. It replaced an earlier mansion that had been burnt down not long after it was visited by Mary Queen of Scots, and it too had replaced another which was destroyed by Niall Stewart of Garth in 1502. The journey to Weem must have seemed to the Queen like a trek to the back of beyond. There was no road up the Tay valley from Dunkeld and no bridge across the river—only ferry boats and swing boats. And down in the Lowlands were folks in high places who could have told you from hearsay of wild goings-on in this district. At the law courts in Edinburgh, some thirty years later, it was recorded that all through the reign of Mary Queen of Scots the region was notorious for sornings and oppressions by the wicked McGregors, and law and order had completely broken down. But that does not seem to have worried her unduly—or the squad of Lowland masons and other craftsmen who arrived a few years later to build the chief's new castle in a fashionable Lowland style.

Though the Queen never saw the present castle, she may have worshipped inside the little church which still stands in the burial ground at Weem, close to the more modern church. It is said to have been built about 1510. A century

St Cuthbert's Cross, on the slabstone in the foreground, may have been carved by the saint himself.

later Sir Alexander Menzies made alterations and improvements, and on the lintel above one of the doors can be seen the initials A.M.—M.C., those of Sir Alexander and his wife Margaret Campbell with the date 1606.

Since the new church was built, this old one has been the burial vault of the Menzies chiefs and their families. And since in the new church they no longer chain their more wayward parishioners to the wall by way of punishment, the jougs still remain in the old one. Decorating the walls are the brightly painted hatchments that were each proudly carried in the funeral procession of some Menzies chief. One of these, still as bright as the day it was painted, is three centuries old. At least a century older is an ornate gravestone on which one of the chiefs is portrayed in armour, with his lady and their numerous family. Far older than it are two cross stones that stand guard over the Menzies graves. They were taken into the chapel about a century ago and they have been described more than once as sanctuary crosses from the old Celtic monastery at Dull. More probably, however, they come from an outlying part of Weem parish, across the river at Newhall, near the standing stones of Croft-moraig. Of them the parish minister, the Rev. Alexander Campbell, wrote in 1840: "There are two upright crosses, close to each other, in the district of Newhall, said to have been the sides of a gateway to a Druidical place of worship at no great distance." Though the crosses are old, they are not as old as the Druids. They are not even as old as a little cross that has been leaning against the wall in the same chapel for the last six years. This is the one which St Cuthbert is said to have carved in his hermitage up on Weem Rock and it is ancient enough for that. It was brought into the old church for safety because vandals were around.

The most remarkable of all the relics in this Menzies vault, however, is a mortuary ornament on the north wall, one of the most ornate of its kind in Scotland. It would be remarkable anywhere but here it is specially so, for it is beautifully carved and in striking contrast to the rough stonework of the rest of the building. Sixteen feet high and twelve feet wide, it was erected in 1616 by the same Sir Alexander Menzies whose initials are outside the door.

Beneath the floor of the little church the

Cosily wrapped in their belted plaids, they await the call to Valhalla.

[105]

A tribute to the ladies of Clan Menzies

Menzies menfolk lie in serried ranks, three abreast, each with a massive slab on top and most with a stone cross on the slab. It is easy to imagine them there at your feet, cosily wrapped in their belted plaids, with their swords and their dirks, waiting expectantly for the skirl of the pipes, to let them cast aside their wearisome slabs and go marching three deep into the banquet hall of their Menzies Valhalla. But the ornate monument on the wall is not in memory of them. It is a tribute to the gentler sex. Sir Alexander erected it in memory of his two wives, his mother, his grandmother, his great-grandmother and his great-great-grandmother.

It was at Weem that the most famous of all Highland regiments, The Black Watch, was embodied in 1740 and the actual beginnings of the regiment go back further still to 1725. Marshal Wade, the army commander-in-chief, came to Weem that year to set up his head-quarters in the village inn, while carrying out the most ambitious plan that had ever been attempted, to subdue the unruly Highlands. By the time it was finished, there was a network of military roads and bridges where there had only been footpaths before. The roads included one through Weem and Coshieville, and over the hills to Rannoch. Among the bridges the most handsome of all was the one which still spans the Tay between Weem and Aberfeldy. In 1968, when the Post Office decided to include four British bridges in a series of pictorial postage stamps, this Wade Bridge at Aberfeldy was chosen to be one of them, the only one from Scotland.

Marshal Wade arrived at Weem only a few years after the Jacobite Rising of 1715, at a time when every Highlander was still acutely feeling the degradation of being forbidden to wear arms, and he used this fact to his advantage. To keep order in the Highlands he formed six Independent Companies. They were given swords, daggers and pistols, they wore the belted plaid, they had officers as Highland as themselves, and they were given a solemn promise that they would never have to serve outside the Highlands. They were merely to keep law and order—to ensure that the clans stayed at peace with each other and stopped their annoying habit of stealing other people's cattle or demanding blackmail from Lowland farmers. It was such a reasonable offer that there was a rush of volunteers. It restored a

"And the greatest of these is Charity."

The bridge which General Wade built still spans the Tay at Aberfeldy

man's dignity to be able to wear arms again.

Those Independent Companies were quite unlike any other troops in Britain, then or since. One English officer wrote in amazement to a friend: "I cannot forbear to tell you that many of those private gentleman-soldiers have gillys, or servants, to attend them in quarters, and upon a march to carry their provisions, baggage and firelocks." It was not officers he was referring to but privates, many of whom were the sons of landowners or gentleman farmers. Even these had little chance of being accepted for service unless they were uncommonly tall, broad and handsome. In the early days, many of them did in fact arrive at the parade ground on horseback, attended by a gillie carrying his gun and uniform.

Most of the companies were stationed in the district where they were raised and for almost fourteen years the Government honoured its promise that they would not be moved out of the Highlands. Their tartans were of sombre colours, mostly black, green and blue, and they did not wear red coats, and so as early as 1737 they were already becoming known unofficially as the Black Watch, in contrast to the Seidar Dearag, the red-coated soldiers of the regular army.

The time came, however, when foreign wars made the Government change its policy and in 1739 a secret decision was made to change the Independent Companies of the Highlands into a regiment of the line. By October that year, the commissions were coming through for the officers. About the same time King George I decided that he would like to see what a Highland soldier looked like, so three of the most handsome of the privates were chosen to make the long journey. One of them suddenly died before he had even left the Highlands but the other two—Gregor McGregor (known as Gregor the Beautiful) and John Campbell of the Perthshire family of Duneaves — arrived in London to give a display before the King in the Great Gallery at St James's Palace. Not only the King was there. So too were most of the high command, including the Duke of Cumberland and Marshal Wade, to see how a Highlander used the broadsword and deadly Lochaber axe. The *Caledonian Mercury* of 21st January 1740 recorded that they "performed their Exercise before his Majesty, the Duke, and general Officers, with such Dexterity that his Majesty ordered them a handsome

It was probably in the early 16th century that this warrior and his lady and their eight young children attended the pre-Reformation church at Weem.

H   [109]

The Black Watch Memorial, Aberfeldy.

Gratuity." The *Westminster Gazette* went into even more detail—"Each got a gratuity of one guinea, which they gave to the porter at the palace gate as they passed out. They thought that the King had mistaken their character and condition in their own country."

A few weeks later the men of the Independent Companies, still unaware of what was in store, were arriving at Weem in their hundreds, from all over the Highlands. And on the bank of the River Tay, in the heart of the Menzies country, they were mustered and embodied into the 43rd Regiment. A handsome memorial, to mark the historic event, was erected in 1887 on the rising ground at the Aberfeldy end of the bridge which Marshal Wade had built. It would not have been possible to erect the monument on the actual site of the muster, in a field at the other end of the bridge at Boltachan, because the river had a habit of overflowing its banks there.

After the muster in 1740, the regiment remained in the district for about fifteen months, while some of the men trained at Taybridge and the others at Point of Lyon. They were issued with a scarlet jacket and waistcoat with buff facings and white lace, and although in their new uniforms those men of the 43rd Regiment lost much of their Black Watch look, the name stuck until eventually it became their official name. With their redcoats too they got a new tartan, designed for the regiment, each man being issued with twelve yards of it for his belted plaid. With the sole exception of the Cameron Highlanders, every Highland regiment wears a variation of this Black Watch tartan.

Although an Englishman had invented the kilt upwards of thirty years before that, the belted plaid was still much more widely worn in the Highlands, by civilians as well as soldiers. You put your belt on the ground, arranged your plaid in pleats on top of it, then lay on your back to fasten the belt. The lower part looked like a kilt, but with pleats all round instead of an apron in front. The upper part could be arranged for freedom or for warmth. And characteristic of the belted plaid was the bulge of material at the back. The belt had a variety of uses. Not only was the plaid tucked into it. It was also used for carrying weapons. You could strengthen your loins by tightening it when you were running up or down hill and everyone knew in those days

that tightening the belt was the easiest way to forget the pangs of hunger. But there was no longer the same need for belt tightening. A soldier's life was happier now than it had ever been in the Independent Companies. The hours were more regular, the pay more certain. There was still no hint that the men would ever be moved out of their native Highlands.

Three years passed and then there was another journey south, under less happy auspices than the one that Gregor McGregor and John Campbell had made. In March 1743 the regiment was assembled at Perth to march into England, they were told, so that they could show themselves to the King. On reaching London, they were reviewed on 14th May by Marshal Wade and then the rumours began to fly. They had been brought south by trickery. The Government thought they were Jacobite rebels. They were going to be shipped off to work in the American plantations. Only death could be worse than that!

It was only too easy for misunderstandings to arise in a regiment where nearly everyone could speak and understand only the Gaelic. Three days after the review, two hundred of them decided that they had seen enough of England. At a smart Highland pace, keeping away from main roads and using the cover of woods wherever possible, they set off on the return journey to their own country and for two days and nights they disappeared. An advertisement was published urging the civil officers to keep a stringent watch for them and by the evening of the second day they were traced. By that time they had reached Northamptonshire. And there, surrounded by cavalry, they eventually laid down their arms. A few weeks later they were lined up on Tower Hill, in London, to watch three of their number being shot as deserters. The sentence caused a wave of indignation and disgust throughout Scotland.

The rest of the regiment were already in Flanders by that time. They fought their first foreign enemy at Fontenoy in May 1745. "The Highland forces rushed in upon us with more violence than ever did a sea driven by a tempest," said a report published in Paris a few days later. One Highland soldier distinguished himself especially in that battle — James Campbell, who killed nine of the enemy with his broadsword. He wanted to fight on longer, but his comrades insisted on leading him away,

A German artist's impression of a Highland officer riding with his wife to battle
on the Continent in 1743.

because a cannon ball had shot off his left arm. The Duke of Cumberland was so moved that he made him a lieutenant for his bravery. And that was the first of the battle honours on which military historians a century later began to build up a nostalgic picture of the traditions of The Black Watch. But in the 1740s people were not specially interested in traditions. The sons of gentleman farmers were no longer flocking to join. Even their gillies were strangely reluctant to do so, after the shooting of the three "deserters".

The army, of course, has changed like everything else since those days. One old feature gone forever is the long procession of camp followers, women and children, who used to trail with the baggage behind the troops, round the battlefields of Europe. They still tramped on, for many a year after the 43rd Regiment was embodied. A German artist has left his impressions of a column of Highland soldiers marching to battle on the Continent in 1743, the year when the 43rd first landed there. The officers were on horseback and one of them, a lieutenant, had his wife riding alongside him. Some of the details — the lieutenant's shield, for example — are not quite as they should be. But he got the general idea. It had been a long and exhausting journey. The officer called for a bottle of wine for his wife and encouraged her with thoughts not of medals and the glory of war but of the booty they were going to take home with them. This, of course, was not necessarily a Black Watch officer. There was more than one Highland regiment on the Continent at that time. He could have been in any Highland regiment — including The Black Watch.

One of the earliest authentic pictures of a soldier in Highland dress, however, is quite definitely of a Black Watch private, depicted scarcely three years after the 43rd Regiment was embodied. He wears the belted plaid and the red coat of a soldier of the line. It was not until about 1814 that the belted plaid was completely ousted by the kilt. And then the time was fast approaching when the perfervid Scot was going to adopt this military garb — a coat with facings and cuffs and lace, and a kilt in a new fangled "clan tartan" — as the national dress of Scotland.

This illustration is not just interesting, however, as a picture of the Black Watch uniform in its earliest days. It is a portrait

The soldier on his pedestal at Aberfeldy wears on his bonnet an eagle's feather, a sure sign that this deserter was a true Highland gentleman.

of a rather special soldier, Pte. Farquhar Shaw, one of the three deserters who were shot on Tower Hill.

Although deserters are not usually regarded as the stuff of British military history, the three who died on Tower Hill have never been forgotten. The Black Watch has always been rather proud of Cpl. Malcolm McPherson, his brother Samuel and Pte. Shaw. Their portraits are in The Black Watch Museum in Perth and the United Services Museum in Edinburgh Castle. And eighty years ago, when it was decided to erect the national monument at Aberfeldy in memory of the founding of the regiment, who better could be chosen for the figure of a soldier, larger than life, on top, than one of the beloved deserters. They chose the private, Farquhar Shaw. A clan chief is entitled to wear three eagle's feathers in his bonnet as a sign of his rank and a chieftain two. Pte. Shaw, on his pedestal, wears the single feather which marks him out as a Highland gentleman.

One of the earliest authentic pictures of a soldier in Highland dress is this one, of
that very special Black Watch private, Farquhar Shaw. There was a wave of Scottish
indignation when he was shot as a deserter in 1743.

One gable-end of Rob Roy's house at Corriechaorach can still be seen on a hillock above the road in Glen Dochart.

7

"The Marveills of the Graves"

LOVELIEST OF ALL the towns of Perthshire is Killin, where the River Dochart comes cascading down its rocky channel to the bridge at Inchbhuidh, *The yellow isle*, and on to Loch Tay. Killin is in the heart of the MacNab country. For centuries the chiefs lived here, and though for a time they lost their ancient inheritance to the Campbells of Glenorchy, now the Campbells are gone and the MacNabs are back. The natives of Killin, however, are cradled in the far more distant past. In the neat white church at the foot of the winding street, the infants of Killin are christened in a huge seven-sided Celtic font that is well over a thousand years old. It is probably the oldest still in use in any Scottish church. When the youngster goes to school, behind the schoolhouse he finds a standing stone that marks the reputed grave where Fionn lies buried. By that time, probably he has also seen the stone circle near Kinnell House and heard of the Yuletide ceremony at the mill, and perhaps heard too of Malice Doire, the farm worker, who guarded a priceless treasure in his cottage just across the bridge. There have been black magic and white magic in and around Killin. And up Glen Dochart in bygone days there was a famous neighbour in Rob Roy McGregor. It was at Corriechaorach that some of his most daring exploits took place.

Only the foundations and one sturdy gable remain of this home of the most famous of the McGregors. It stands in the shadow of a pylon on the hillside some eight miles west of Killin, at the foot of Ben More on the road to Crianlarich. Alex McLaggan, the Dalmally coachman, used to tell his tourists as he took them past the house: "That's one of the places where Rob Roy was born." But it wasn't. Until he was about forty his Glen Dochart home was at Portnellan, about four miles away, near Loch Dochart and its ruined castle. He was still there in 1711, when his speculations in the cattle trade were heading for disaster. In 1712 the Duke of Montrose seized his estates farther south, as security for unpaid debts, and from then on Glen Dochart saw more of him than it had ever done before. It was then that he moved to Corriechaorach. But he still spent many an evening in the inns at Crianlarich and Tyndrum.

He was a giant of a man, tall and broad and red-haired, with arms so long that he could tie his garters without even stooping. And that tremendous reach helped to make him a formidable swordsman. Graham of Killearn, the Duke of Montrose's factor, discovered this to his cost when with a band of troops he cornered him, one night, in the old inn at Crianlarich. Twenty of McGregor's followers were asleep in the barn, but Graham locked the barn door and mounted a guard outside, then brought the rest of his men to the inn to make the arrest. But he forgot how narrow the door was. Only one could get through at a time and soon there were five lying wounded in a heap in the doorway. Then the men in the barn got their door burst open and soon they had their leader safely out of reach.

He was not always fighting against odds, however. It was his practical jokes more than anything else that made him the legendary figure he became. The inn at Tyndrum was one of the places remembered for that. When the hunt for him was at its height, an officer and forty men arrived at the inn, in search of him. Disguised as a beggar, he slouched into the kitchen where the men were gathered and let them know that he could take them to the outlaw's house. He proved to be an excellent guide, so considerate that when they found the Fillan Water in spate at Dalrie ford, he carried them over one by one, and occasionally two by two. He had won golden opinions by the time they were past Crianlarich and on to within sight of Corriechaorach. Now, he warned them, was the time for guile. He would go ahead to allay suspicion and then, two at a time, they would come up and into the house, until there were enough to seize all those inside. And so he disarmed the lot. Next morning he gave them a good breakfast and sent them off on their return journey, without a weapon among them.

It is not recorded whether it happened in 1725. But 1725 was a year when he had more weapons than he knew what to do with. That was the year when Parliament passed an Act making it unlawful for Highlanders to bear

Rob Roy's grave in Balquhidder Churchyard.

Inchbuidh has a "watcher" system.

arms, and Marshal Wade sent one of his colonels to Finlarig Castle to collect all the arms in the district. No one came from Rannoch and very few from Atholl. In fact, the only ones who came in any numbers from the whole of Highland Perthshire were the McGregors. About forty of them came marching through Killin and up to the castle, with a piper out in front and Rob Roy's eldest son just behind, and Rob Roy himself in the company, to surrender their arms. And then he returned to his lawless ways. As time went on, he found even Glen Dochart too unsafe. He moved south across the hills to the lonely farm of Inverlochlarig Beag, at the back of beyond, six miles west of Balquhidder Church along the braes, and there he died at the end of 1734. As he lay on his deathbed he renounced all his un-Christian deeds and became a Roman Catholic. He even forgave his enemies at the priest's urgent demand. And as he forgave them he turned his piercing eye on his son Robin Og. "Look you to them," he hissed.

He was very near to death when one of the damned MacLarens came to see him, so the household had to get him out of bed and wrap him in his plaid and prop him up in his armchair by the fire. They forgot about his weapons but he reminded them. And there like a warrior chief he sat and talked with MacLaren. When their business was done and the man was away, he called for his piper to play a lament and he was dead before it was ended.

They buried him just across from the door of old Balquhidder Church. On one side of him lies his wife Helen and on the other side his sons Coll and Robin Og. Robin's body was brought from Edinburgh for burial, after he had been hanged in the Grassmarket. But it was not seeing to his father's enemies that was the death of him. He was condemned for helping to abduct a girl.

Rob Roy was not by any means the only giant among men who lived around Killin. Finlarig Castle, on one side of the Dochart as it enters Loch Tay, has memories of Black Duncan Campbell of Glenorchy, "Black Duncan of the Cowl," with his gory execution pit. And in Kinnell House, just across the Dochart, there lived two centuries ago another famous figure, one of the lords of creation, the legendary Francis MacNab of MacNab, 16th chief of his line. Raeburn painted his portrait. Lesser mortals wove legends round him. A visitor to Killin in 1816 was shown the burial place of the MacNabs on the island of Inch-bhuidh. "I was told," said this awe-struck tourist, "that in the same burying-ground about

For at least a century St Fillan's healing stones have been kept behind these iron bars in a niche in the old mill wall at Killin.

thirty of the wives of the present MacNab lay buried. It is said he has more children than any man in Scotland; and that amongst his fair promises to each succeeding bride is that of there being secured to her a place in the prettiest burying-ground in the whole country." But the visitor had not got the story quite right. Later that year, when Francis MacNab of MacNab was laid to rest in the little walled enclosure beside his ancestors, he was still a bachelor. He had twice come near to matrimony. In 1786, when he was on the other side of fifty, a certain Janet Buchanan tried to get her daughter legally recognised as his wife. But she was unsuccessful. Another time he did in fact try to get a girl to marry him, with a promise that she would be buried on lovely Inchbhuidh. But she refused the laird, with a' that. Maybe she had heard something else about this burial place of the MacNabs. It has a "watcher" system. The last person buried keeps watch over all the rest, until there is another funeral and a new watcher takes over. It was a sobering thought for any young lassie, of high or low degree.

The little vault on Inchbhuidh has been the burial place of the chiefs of Clan MacNab for at least four centuries but the history of the clan goes back far beyond that. They trace their origin to the lay abbots of Glen Dochart and further still to the days of St Fillan, thirteen hundred years ago. For a time they lost their lands, for fighting against King Robert the Bruce, but they were back in possession a few years later, when David II gave Gilbert McNab a charter of Bovain, on the north side of the glen a few miles above Killin.

By the early sixteenth century the chiefs were in financial troubles and already they were becoming heavily involved with the Campbells of Glenorchy. But the less money they had, the more colourful they seemed to become. There was "Smooth John" MacNab, for example, in the mid-seventeenth century. He and his brothers could all drive their dirks through a two-inch board. John was the leader of a band of MacNabs who carried a boat over the hills to Loch Earn and sailed across the water to massacre the Nishes on the Isle of Loch Earn. That is why the MacNabs have a boat and Nish's head on their armorial bearings.

The MacNab castle at that time was Ellanryne, less than half-a-mile from Finlarig Castle, on the east bank of the river. But it was burned by the English a few years later, in 1654, and Kinnell House then became the home of the chiefs. That was where Francis MacNab lived like a feudal prince, surrounded by faithful retainers and the mountains of debt he bequeathed to his nephew Archibald, the 17th chief. There was a famous seer, the Lady of Lawers, who predicted that when the broken branch of a fir tree was blown on to another fir and became grafted to it, the MacNabs would lose their lands to the Campbells of Glenorchy. And that happened while Archibald was chief. Overwhelmed with debts and with the Earl of Breadalbane his biggest creditor, he fled to Canada in 1823 to escape the debtors' prison. And there he was treated like a chief again. He persuaded the Governor-General to give him 80,000 acres of land, so that he could bring his clansmen across from Glen Dochart, and about eighty-five of them — men, women and children — came across to make a little corner of Scotland on the banks of the Ottawa River. He lived as a chief among them, until thirteen years later the Canadian Government held an inquiry. Then it was established that all this time the clansmen had been paying MacNab a rent for land which in fact was free. There were other irregularities too. MacNab was ordered to re-compense them and that put him £35,000 in debt. His ancestral estates in Scotland were sold in 1828 to the 4th Earl of Breadalbane.

The MacNabs are back in Kinnell House. It was repurchased by the late Archibald MacNab, who became 22nd chief in 1955. And now the lands of Finlarig, so long possessed by the Campbells, are again back in the hands of the McNabs — all except the overgrown enclosure that contains the Campbells' castle and their burial vault. The grafted branch on the fir tree on Inchbuidh, the branch to which the Lady of Lawers referred, was still growing when the lands were repurchased. It has withered and died since then.

It was not a MacNab, however, or a Campbell or even Rob Roy who made the most lasting impression on this district. It was a priest, St Fillan, who lived several miles up the glen, twelve centuries ago, in a chapel beyond Crianlarich. The *Buidhean*—the Struan bell which became fixed to a rock on the Hill of Bohespie — was said to be one of his relics. Killin has its relics too. Beside the Falls of Dochart is St Fillan's Mill and in its gable wall is a niche with iron bars. On a bed of rushes in the niche are eight water-worn stones, two of which seem to have been used at one time as sockets for the spindle of an upper mill-

St Fillan's healing stones.

The Quigrich, the ancient shrine which contains the crozier head of St Fillan.

stone. These eight stones are known as St Fillan's healing stones.

Each was for a particular part of the body. For mental troubles and pains in the head, one was used that is shaped like a head, with two highly polished holes forming the eyes and a mouth cut in the stone. Another, with a single hole, was for breast ailments. For pains in the back there was one with marks like the joints of the backbone. Another, flat and round, was for the stomach. And there were stones for each side of the body, with lines on them like ribs. In the early nineteenth century the keeper of the stones was an old woman. She rubbed them round the affected part three times one way, three times the other and three times the first way again, while she recited a Gaelic benediction. Hers was a hereditary office which was said to have been held for centuries by her ancestors. And in her day the Presbyterian minister of Killin had no doubt that the stones were out of the ordinary. In the *New Statistical Account* he referred to them as "seven small round stones which had been consecrated by the saint and endowed with the power of curing diseases. Each of them had its peculiar merit." He used the past tense, for there were only five stones there when he was writing. But there is an old tradition that the stones are endowed with the power to return of their own accord if they are taken away. And that seems in fact to have happened. Now there are quite definitely eight! And that has been their number all through this century.

There is an annual ceremony connected with those stones. Each Christmas Eve the keeper, the owner of the mill, goes down to the river bank to gather rushes that have been washed up. They must not on any account be cut. He takes them to the mill, removes the bed of rushes on which the stones have been lying for the past twelve months and substitutes this new bed for the ensuing year. Though it is a long time since the stones have been used for healing, the ceremony of changing the bed still continues.

And something else has continued too for many a long year. On St Fillan's Day, 20th January, no one must on any account work in the mill. It is still believed that ill luck would befall anyone who broke that rule.

The healing stones at Killin are not the only ones in the district. Two miles away, on the

[122]

shore of Loch Tay below Morenish, is Cladh Dhavi, a burial ground of the McDiarmids. Two stones were kept there as an infallible cure for breast troubles. Years ago a new tenant moved into a neighbouring farm and, knowing nothing about the stones, carried them off to be ornaments outside his front door. Soon the Marchioness of Breadalbane arrived in person to make sure that they went back on to the gravestone where they belonged.

In bygone days you could have seen in Killin a relic of St Fillan that was even more famous than his healing stones. The Quigrich used to be kept in a cottage in Gray Street, just across the river from the mill. Now one of the more special treasures in the Scottish National Museum of Antiquities, it has a quite unusual history. When St Fillan was living in this district he is believed to have had a wooden crozier, which was preserved as a relic after his death. About the ninth century its wooden head is said to have been encased in bronze, covered with ornate panels of silver filigree, and so it continued for the next five centuries. Then, about the fourteenth century, a new and very handsome case was made. Of silver-gilt, it had the figure of a churchman—probably of St Fillan himself—in front, and beneath the figure was a large oval crystal, reminiscent of the charm stones we have met before. To complete the decoration, the fine old panels of silver filigree were transferred from the copper head on to the sides of this new case. The original wooden crozier has long since disappeared but the ninth century head and the fourteenth century case still survive.

This Quigrich has a well documented antiquity. In 1336, only 22 years after the battle of Bannockburn, its custodian was Donald McSobrell, who held part of the lands of Ewich in Strathfillan. A century later the custodian was Finlay Jore (The word *jore* or *doire* or *dewar* means "custodian"). On 2nd April 1428 a court was held in Killin to establish whether being custodian involved him in any special duties and the court found that it did. They heard evidence that one of Finlay's ancestors was given custody of the relic by a successor of St Fillan and in every King's reign from Robert the Bruce onwards, the Jore was entitled to an annual supply of meal from each inhabitant of the parish. In return, if any of them " has any goods or chattels stolen and dares not go in pursuit, through doubt about

The crozier head of St Fillan.

the culprit or tribal feuds, he may send a message to the Jore of the Coygerach, with fourpence or a pair of shoes and food for one night, and thereupon the Jore is at his own expense to go in pursuit, wherever he can find a path within the Kingdom of Scotland."

In 1487 one of Finlay's descendants received a letter from James III under the Privy Seal, confirming that as far as the relic was concerned the Doire was answerable only to the King and anyone hindering him while he journeyed with it was liable to the "hiest pain". In 1734, at the instance of Malice Doire, this letter was registered in Edinburgh as a probative writ.

The Doires were probably one of the leading families in Glen Dochart, when they became the guardians of the Quigrich, but as the centuries passed they lost their social standing, though they still retained the relic. In the reign of Charles II they lost it too for a time. They were Protestant then and a Catholic relic was scarcely suitable for a Protestant family. They sold it to the Roman Catholic McDonells of Glengarry. But there were "evil consequences". They got it back some years later.

We next hear of it in July 1782, when an Oxford graduate, a William Thompson, arrived in Killin while touring Scotland. He heard so much about the relic that he went to see its envied possessor, Malice Doire. He saw the royal letter and he discovered that Malice was a day labourer. He also saw the presumptive heir to the treasure, a nineteen-year-old youth, who was lying "drooping in an outer apartment under the last gasp of a consumption."

Thirteen years later a French refugee, the amusing M. de Latocnaye, also saw the relic in Killin. He noticed that the Doire was not only collecting fees for exhibiting it but was using the crystal as a cattle cure. It was specially potent for animals that became too wild. Water was poured through the inside of the relic and then given to the beast to drink. But first a little of the healing water was poured on the ground. If it was not going to work, it boiled on the ground, the Frenchman was told. "From which fact," he pithily observed, "one may conclude that it often works."

"It charmed me," he added, "to find a relic among the Presbyterians." But superstitions in those days were sometimes stronger than religious convictions.

The Quigrich passed from Malice to his younger brother Alexander, who encouraged visitors to come and see it as "one of the greatest pieces of antiquity in Scotland". In 1808 he took it to Edinburgh and there he put it on show for several days, from 10 a.m. to 4 p.m., with an admission fee of two shillings. Ten years later the guardian was his son Archibald, who emigrated to Canada and took it with him to a remote prairie clearing. There it remained for many years, until Archibald's son Alexander transferred it for safer keeping to the strong room of a Canadian Custom House. By that time he was willing to sell it for £500 but no one was willing to pay so much.

During all the time it was in his possession it was only twice used for the cure of cattle and he never tried to find out whether it did them any good. He knew, however, that in Killin it had been used for people too. In a letter to a University professor he wrote: "It was regarded as an effectual cure for fever, by administering, or sprinkling with water in which it had been dipped; and was no less infallible in cases of scrofula, or the King's evil, by being rubbed on the affected parts." This Alexander Dewar was the last of the hereditary custodians. In 1877, when he was in his 87th year, a settlement was reached and it was sent back to Scotland, to the National Museum of Antiquities.

At one time there are believed to have been not just one but five Doires in the district, each the custodian of a relic of St Fillan, and certainly in 1541 there were still three—"Malice Doir of Quickrich, Archibald Doir of Fergy and Malcolm Doir Bernane." A lawsuit provides proof of that. With the Reformation approaching, the prior of Strathfillan decided that the holy relics would be safer in his keeping and he threatened to excommunicate the three Doires unless they handed over their relics. When they still refused, he took legal action against them and the court upheld their claim to be the rightful guardians. He was forbidden to harm them in any way.

No one now knows what the Fergy was but it might have been an arm bone of the saint. There is an old tradition that when he was working in his cell at Strathfillan, one night, a servant came to call him to supper. Noticing a brilliant light streaming through a chink in the door, the man put his eye to the hole. And inside he saw St Fillan, with his pen in one hand and his other hand held high. He was writing by

St Fillan's Chapel, Glen Dochart.

St Fillan's Magic Pool

Until recently the boulder still lay in the middle of the chapel. But latterly the cattle kept knocking it over, so it was moved into a corner.

the nuptial ceremony; the direction in which they go at least half round the grave before the coffin is deposited; the direction in which they go round any consecrated fountain whose waters are supposed to have some medicinal virtues . . . This custom they call the Lucky or Fortunate Way of turning round, and the opposite direction is the Ominous or Unfortunate Way." You had to be sure you went the Lucky Way round the cairns at the pool.

In all this the pool was no different from many other holy places in the Highlands and the Lowlands. But in the ritual for madness St Fillan's treatment was unique. It took place between dusk and sunrise. Just after dark the patient was immersed in the water with a rope tied round his waist. Then he was brought out with his nine stones. After going round the cairns and leaving the stones and his bonnet there, he was taken a mile down the river bank to St Fillan's ruined chapel, when the second part of the ceremony was now about to begin. On the flat stone in the middle of the chapel was the old Celtic bell and beside the bell was a schistose boulder with a deeply cut hollow. shaped like a heart. A wooden framework was there as well. The framework was used to tie the patient down to the stone, with his head in

the hollow of the boulder. And then the bell was placed on his head. Covered with hay he was left like that for the rest of the night. As dawn approached, the relatives returned and their eyes went immediately to the ropes. If these were loose, there was every chance of a cure. If they were still tight, one could only try again.

That English tourist who came in 1798 had heard — and so of course had everyone in the district — that, if anyone stole the bell, like St Fillan's healing stones it would return of its own accord. It would come back "ringing all the way". But by that time it had lost its homing instinct. The Englishman stole the bell that day and took it home with him, and it was kept in his family for seventy years before it was brought back to Scotland to find a place alongside the Quigrich in the National Museum of Antiquities. But though the bell was missing the rest of the ritual still carried on, far into the nineteenth century.

In the year 1862 one of Scotland's leading antiquarians, Professor J. Y. Simpson, wrote a paper for the Society of Antiquaries of Scotland in which he said: "I was lately informed by the Rev. Mr Stewart of Killin that in one of the last cases so treated—and that only a few years ago—the patient was found sane in the morning and unbound; a dead relative, according to the patient's own account, having entered the church during the night and loosened her both from the ropes that bound her body and the delusions that warped her mind."

Coming from a Presbyterian minister that might seem to be no small tribute. But Highland ministers, like Highland folk in general, were not too anxious in those days to dogmatize on the supernatural. Dr Robertson of Callander was no exception when he wrote, upwards of two centuries ago, about another old Highland belief: "I am not very superstitious nor much inclined to give credit to tales about hob-goblins, yet I cannot forbear to mention what a man of veracity told me not long ago . . . " Sometimes it was not easy to know what to believe.

*   *   *

Before we finish there is still one more strange fact to be recorded. Since we left Glenlyon we have gone by Rannoch and Tummel and Blair Atholl, by Weem and Kenmore and Loch Tay, by Killin and on to Strathfillan. And in our travels we have come across many an old tested remedy for the ills of the flesh—the charm stones that the lairds possessed, the healing stones at Killin and Morenish, the stones where the rain water gathered to cure your whooping cough or measles, the specialist springs that were famous remedies for toothache or fever, sciatica, scrofula, gravel and many other individual ailments. A veritable pharmacopoeia was there, to heal all the ills of man and beast, from the cradle to the shadow of the grave, and many of these carried the blessing of a saint. The healing stones at Killin were St Fillan's, the spring on Weem Rock was St Cuthbert's, the one at Dull was Eonan's.

And yet the odd thing is that in the one place where other traditions have lingered on most strongly, in Glenlyon, you can search from end to end in vain for a whooping cough stone, a specialist spring or a healing stone. Though it carries so many memories of Eonan, it seems to have inherited none of his remedies. Maybe to him it was a sort of Shangri-la at the back of beyond that needed no mundane remedies.

The Bernane

The Guthrie Bell

The Kilmichael Glassary Bell and Shrine.

Although none of the Celtic bells of Perthshire is enclosed in a shrine, two others from the West of Scotland show by their lavish decoration how much those bells were venerated. The Guthrie Bell has its 12th and 15th century ornamentation on the bell itself. The Kilmichael Glassary Bell was enclosed in its handsome shrine towards the end of the 12th century and underneath a hole was provided, through which the devout could touch the actual bell.

A READING LIST

Anon: *Strath Fillan & Glen Dochart in bygone days* (Stirling 1911).

Campbell, Duncan: *The Book of Garth & Fortingall*. Printed for private circulation (Inverness 1888).

Campbell, Duncan: *The Lairds of Glenlyon* (Perth 1886).

Campbell, John Gregorson: *Superstitions of the Highlands and Islands of Scotland* (Glasg. 1900).

Dunbar, John Telfer: *History of Highland Dress* (Edin. 1962).

Dunbar, Rev. R. G.: *A few notes on the Parish of Weem* (Edin. 1897). Microfilmed by Scottish Central Library 1968).

Gillies, Wm. A.: *In Famed Breadalbane* (Perth 1938).

Innes, C. (ed.): *The Black Book of Taymouth,* including the Dean of Lismore's Chronicle of Fortingall. Bannatyne Club (Edin. 1855).

Kennedy, Rev. Dr. J.: *Old Highland Days* (Lond. 1901).

Kermack, W. R.: *The Clan Macgregor* (Edin. 1953).

Latocnaye, M. de: *Promenade autour de la Grande Bretagne* (Edin. 1795).

MacGregor, A. G. M.: *History of the Clan Gregor* (Edin. 1898).

Mackay, Norman D.: *Aberfeldy Past and Present* (Aberfeldy 1955).

McLaggan, Rev. James: *An Account of the Parish of Blair Atholl, in a letter to the Rev. James Scott, Nov. 24, 1786.* MS. No. 42, Lib. Perth Lit. & Ant. Society [In Sandeman Public Library, Perth].

Macwilliam, H. D. (ed.): *The Black Watch Mutiny Records* (Lond. 1910).

Millar, A. H.: *Historical Castles and Mansions of Scotland* (Paisley 1890).

Moncreiffe of that Ilk & David Hicks: *The Highland Clans* (Lond. 1967).

Pennant, Thomas: *A Tour in Scotland*. 1769 (Chester 1771).

Pitcairn, Robert, W.S.: *Criminal Trials in Scotland,* vol. ii McGregor trials). Bannatyne Club (Edin. 1833).

Register of the Privy Council of Scotland, vols. iii-xi, for references to Clan Gregor in introduction and text (Edin. 1880-94).

Robertson, D.: *A brief account of the Clan Donnachaidh with notes on its history and traditions* (Glasg. 1894).

Robertson, Rev. J.: *General View of the Agriculture in the County of Perth* (Perth 1813).

Root, Margt. E.: *Dunkeld Cathedral Official Guide-Book* (H.M.S.O. 1965)

Scott, Sir Walter: Introduction to "*Rob Roy*".

The Statistical Account of Scotland: Perthshire parishes (Edin. 1791-9).

New Statistical Account of Scotland: Perthshire (Edin. 1845).

Stewart, Alexander: *A Highland Parish, or The History of Fortingall etc.* (Glasg. 1928).

Stewart, Major-Gen. David: *Sketches of the Highlanders of Scotland*. 2 vols. (Edin. 1822).

Victoria, Queen of Great Britain & Ireland: *Leaves from the Journal of our Life in the Highlands.*

ARTICLES

Anderson, Dr. Joseph: *Notices of the Quigrich or Crozier and other relics of St. Fillan in the possession of their hereditary keepers or Dewars in Glendochart in 1549–50.* Proceedings of the Society of Antiquaries of Scotland, xxiii 110-118 (Edin. 1889).

Anon: *Early Celtic Bells in Perthshire (Struan, Clach Bhrennu, Fortingall, Balnahanait).* P.S.A.S. xiii 345-7 (Edin. 1879).

Anon: *Notes on St. Fillan's Priory and Churchyard.* P.S.A.S. xxxii. 121 (Edin. 1898). Also P.S.A.S. xii 134-182 (Edin. 1877).

Anon: *St Cuthbert's Connection with Weem.* P.S.A.S. l 296-302 (Edin. 1916).

Cash, C. G.: *Archaeological Gleanings from Aberfeldy.* P.S.A.S. xlv 386-395 (Edin. 1911).

Cash, C. G.: *Archaeological Gleanings from Killin.* P.S.A.S. xlvi 264-285 (Edin. 1912).

Forbes, Right Rev. Bishop A. P.: *Notice of the ancient Bell of St. Fillan.* P.S.A.S. viii 265-272 (Edin. 1870). [The reference in this article to a phallic symbol on the bell is not now regarded as correct].

Geddes, Rev. Bishop J.: *Some account of a Royal Hunting in the Forest of Atholl in 1563.* Transactions of the Society of Antiquaries of Scotland, ii 111-115 (Edin. 1818).

Gift of Donald Macdonald as a perpetual servant to the Earl of Tullibardine, 5th Dec. 1701. MS No. 22 Lib. Perth Lit. & Ant. Society [In Sandeman Public Library, Perth].

Gow, J. M.: *Holiday notes in Athole, Perthshire, 1889.* P.S.A.S. xxiv 382-7 (Edin. 1890).

Macfarlane Geographical Collection, i & ii. Scottish History Society (Edin. 1906).

Munro, Mrs Jean, Ph.D.: *The Homes of Clan Donnachaidh.* 1965 Clan Donnachaidh Annual.

Porteous, Rev. H.: *Extracts from a history of the parishes of Monivaird and Strowan.* T.S.A.S. ii 65-75 (Edin. 1818).

Robertson, Rev. James, D.D.: *Superstitions of the Highlands, 1791.* Archaeologia Scottica iii 223-7 (Edin. 1831).

Simpson, Dr. J. Y.: *Notes on Some Scottish Magical Charm-Stones.* P.S.A.S. iv 211-224 (Edin. 1862).

Stewart, Dr J.: *Historical Notices of St Fillan's Crozier.* P.S.A.S. xii 134-182 (Edin. 1877).

Walker, J. R.: *Holy Wells in Scotland.* P.S.A.S. xvii 152-210 (Edin. 1883).

Watson, Professor W. J.: *The Circular Forts of North Perthshire.* P.S.A.S. xlvii 30-60 (Edin. 1913).

Watson, Professor W. J.: *Circular Forts in Lorn and North Perthshire.* P.S.A.S. xlix 17-32 (Edin. 1915).

Watson, Professor W. J.: *Circular Forts in Perthshire*. Transactions of Gaelic Society of Inverness, xxviii 151-155 (1918).

Wilson, Dr Daniel: *Notices of the Quigrich or Crozier of St Fillan and its hereditary keepers*. P.S.A.S. xii 122-131 (Edin. 1877).

Wilson, Dr Daniel: *The Quigrich*. Read before the Canadian Institute, 12th February, 1859. The Canadian Journal, New Series, No. xxiv, pp. 429-441—November 1859.

TAPE RECORDING

Ross, Dr Anne: *A Preliminary Survey of the Traditions of Lochtayside and the Parish of Fortingall*. Talk recorded in 1964 by School of Scottish Studies, University of Edinburgh.

POETRY REFERENCES

"The Song of Weem." Translated from the Gaelic by Principal Shairp of St Andrews University and published in *"A Few Notes on the Parish of Weem,"* by Rev. R. G. Dunbar (1897).

"Albin and the daughter of Mey". Translated from the Gaelic by Jerome Stone and published in Scots Magazine, vol. xviii (1756).

INDEX